Elaine,
Fellow Princess
Warrior Goddess!

xoxo,

FROM
C-STUDENT
TO the
C-SUITE

How I Use My Emotional Intelligence
to Gain Access to the Most Influential
People in the world, Even with
All My Sh#t and Insecurities.

-TAMI HOLZMAN-

THIS BOOK HAS BEEN RATED

| FU | FOR FOUL LANGUAGE AND |
| | UNSATISFACTORY BEHAVIOR |
| IRREVERENT HUMOR THROUGHOUT |

= By =

The Holzman Hustle Association

fromcstudenttothecsuite.com

LIONCREST
PUBLISHING

FROM C-STUDENT TO THE C-SUITE
How I Use My Emotional Intelligence to Gain Access to the Most
Influential People in the World, Even with All My Shit and Insecurities.

Edited by: Brooke White
Illustrated and designed by: Rocío Hedman

ISBN: 978-1-61961-412-3
Ebook ISBN: 978-1-61961-413-0

I dedicate this book to *my family & to my best friends (you know who you are).*

I wouldn't have anything to write without all of you in my life. At one time or another, you have all been the Ethel to my Lucy (even if you're a boy).

You've all tilted your heads and wondered "WTF" at some of the surprises I've thrown your way, but in the end, you always let me be myself.

You are the bricks to my foundation, you are the oxygen I breathe, you are the beating of my heart.

ThANK YOU *for being as fabulous and dysfunctional as I and for being my Team Tami champions.*

Contents

CHAPTER 4: GETTING IN: **NO MEETING = NO CHOOS**

CHAPTER 5: KEEPIN' IT REAL

CHAPTER 6: THE FLUFFER

CHAPTER 10: NEUROTI-CUTE: **UNDERSTANDING YOUR SHIT**

CHAPTER 11: BOARDROOM BROAD

CHAPTER 12: PERCEPTION IS REALITY

INTRODUCTION

Are You a Princess Warrior Goddess?

ARE YOU INTIMIDATED BY **TALKING** TO *influential people?*

Do you wonder if people will **like you?**

ARE YOU AFRAID to use your *femininity?*

ARE YOU TALENTED ENOUGH?

Do you question your capabilities?

Do you make an *impression* WHEN YOU WALK INTO A ROOM?

DO YOU WATCH PEOPLE FROM AFAR *instead of participating* in the **conversation?**

DO YOU SECOND-GUESS YOURSELF?

Are you **VULNERABLE?**

Have you ever **felt** like ANOTHER GIRL THREW HER STILETTO *at your forehead?*

IS IT OKAY TO BE **A PARTY GIRL?**

DO YOU THINK OTHERS ARE JUDGING **YOU,** OR ARE YOU **JUDGING THEM?**

IS BUSINESS A POPULARITY CONTEST? *and, if so,* how can you **win?**

Do you think **looks matter?**

Do you think you are **smart enough?**

DO YOU NEED VALIDATION?

Are you **SCARED** OF REJECTION?

Do **you** have **WRINKLES?** *or* "LAUGH LINES"?

Can you be **SUCCESSFUL** *by* BEING YOURSELF?

DO YOU HAVE FUN AT WORK?

DO YOU GET HIT ON At BUSINESS functions?

Can you **get the meeting?**

If you've ever asked yourself any of these questions (or you've questioned yourself), guess what? You should have, because everyone else does. You're normal. The people who never question themselves are the ones who are totally fucked up.

This book is going to show you how, by being your authentic self, you can be successful at selling anything—all while you enjoy the journey and laugh your ass off at my expense (and maybe at your own). Inside, you'll find it all: takeaways, tips, truths, success stories, failures, insecurities, and crazy shenanigans (think Lucille Ball in *I Love Lucy*).

You will be able to analyze your strengths and weaknesses, and you will begin to understand your psyche and come to terms with your true self. There's no lecturing. This is not a textbook (snooze). This is an irreverent book with a no-holds-barred approach to getting in the C-Suite, regardless of your credentials or your GPA. You are going to have FUN! We're on this wacky ride together.

After stumbling across an article in *Forbes* about EQ vs. IQ, I learned that 85% of getting business is due to emotional intelligence—the ability to understand people and customers. The remaining 15% is due to knowledge of the product. When I read that, I breathed a sigh of relief. I've spent most of my life worrying I wasn't smart enough to play in the same sandbox with the high-level muckety-mucks and questioned how I ever got to be successful! As you'll see in the chapters ahead, having a high EQ is a huge advantage when building and sustaining relationships with your BFFs (Business Friends Forever) and creating memories that you'll take to the grave!

Encouraged by a former colleague, I decided to share my stories about business development and some of my adventures in forming rock-solid relationships with countless members of the C-Suite and securing multi-million dollar deals. The reality is, who gives a shit how smart you are if you can't get into the room? And the beauty is, getting there is half the fun.

CHAPTER 1

FUCK HARVARD

A C-STUDENT iN the C-SUiTE

The "C-Suite" is a slang term that refers to a corporation's most important, high-level executives. "C" is for Chief: chief executive officer, chief operating officer, chief financial officer, chief marketing officer, chief brand officer, and so on. The C-Suite is unquestionably the most influential group of individuals within a company. Being a member of this group comes with some high-stakes decision-making[1] (and a pretty fat paycheck).

Hello CEO! We've got something in common, you and me. I represent a different brand of "C"—the perpetual "C" student. For me, it started in high school and lasted all the way until I almost graduated from college. It's pretty hard to shed the C-student skin, but in the real world, personality wins over GPA any day.

In high school, I didn't excel in much of anything. I watched my fellow students furiously scribbling notes and wondered what it was all about. It bothered me that I wasn't good in school (but not enough to actually study). I preferred to go to the mall with my girlfriends, flirt with boys, and play drinking games on the weekends. Many of the social skills gathered in these pursuits wound up contributing to my eventual success in the boardroom, but certainly not in the traditional sense.

I read the textbooks and sometimes did the homework, but I remembered nothing! I didn't like to memorize facts and figures. I wasn't even a good test taker—I could psych myself out of the right answer. My grades were consistent "C"s and "U"s, which stood for average intelligence and unsatisfactory behavior, usually because I was talking too much.

The way I see it, in real life, a U translates to an A+. The sys-

---

1   http://www.investopedia.com/terms/c/c-suite.asp

tem is all fucked up. I'm sure I was talking or socializing too much, but now I get paid the big bucks in business development to do just that! If socializing was my weakness according to my teachers, I say there's an opportunity to capitalize on our weaknesses.

Relationship skills help people to become successful and to understand what makes other people tick. There should be a required class in all high schools where kids connect and just come together to play games, look at art, talk about pop culture, make funny videos, laugh and joke around. It should be mandatory. Wouldn't it be great to see an A, B, C, and D student go into business together? They would kick ass!

It was Einstein who said, "It's a miracle that curiosity survives formal education." People who take chances and have an active imagination are the real winners. Einstein and I, we agree on that.

So, I didn't get into Harvard. The C-U combination just wasn't what they were looking for. Not surprisingly, my college grades continued to sweep the Cs (grades—not the Suite). Nevertheless, I donned the cap and gown, walked the stage, had my photo taken, and went out for the celebration dinner. As a graduation gift, I even backpacked around Europe for three months as a rite of passage to adulthood. There was just one small glitch: my diploma was blank. I was three measly math credits short of my degree, so technically, I'm a college dropout. (Shhh.)

I vividly remember calling my Mom from San Diego State University, crying and saying, "I am coming home to finish school at California State University, Northridge (my 4th College). If I stay here, I'll never graduate!" (And I was right. You can't get a degree in partying.)

Check out Robert Kiyosaki's *Why A Students Work for C Students and Why B Students Work for the Government*. It's brilliant. His whole philosophy is centered on the belief that the school system was created to churn out "E"s, or employees—not creative thinkers. And yet it's the creatives who are the innovators, the entrepreneurs, and ultimately, the moneymakers. I know if my successes in life were directly correlated with my successes in school, I would be screwed. Luckily, I found an inroad to the C-Suite despite the GPA—my personality. Take that, Harvard.

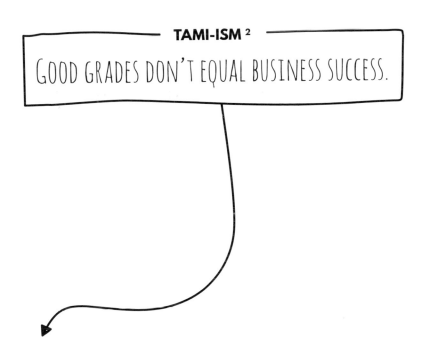

TAMI-ISM [2]

GOOD GRADES DON'T EQUAL BUSINESS SUCCESS.

---

2   "Tami-isms" represent the truths, tips, and takeaways I have uncovered through a lot of trial and error. They're at the end of every section - the "CliffsNotes" for those of you who can't, or won't, or don't want to read a WHOLE book. I get it. And for those of you who simply cannot concentrate at all, there is a complete cheat sheet at the end of the book.

ALL in the FAMILY

I don't mean to sell my Brothers out, but since I am shitting on my own academic journey, it's worth mentioning that they were average students, too. None of us performed well in school, but my twin Brother is now the chief digital officer of a major global media company, and my older Brother is a successful lawyer. We must be doing something right!

While pow-wowing with one of my Brothers about work recently, he said, "You know, the reason we're all such hustlers in business is because school didn't come easy for us. We had to fight for it, and we still fight for credibility to prove something. Being academically challenged made us hungry." I completely agree.

When my older Brother was getting ready to go to law school, he was really scared. He started seeing a therapist to face his fear, and told him, "I am not sure law school is for me." The therapist said, "Why not?" My Brother said, "Well, I barely graduated from college." The therapist said, "Then you will barely graduate from law school." Well, isn't that encouraging? Hell yeah! I love that story!! And you know what? My Brother survived. He got through it, he's an insanely successful lawyer, and he's living proof of the Holzman Hustle. We've all managed to come out on top by sheer strength of will.

 C-STUDENTS FIGHT HARDER.

EXPERIENCE OVER EDUCATION

"Educating the mind without educating the heart
is no education at all."
—ARISTOTLE

I am not discrediting academic achievement (I envy it), but I can promise you—it's not the be all and end all. On the contrary, your drive to make a difference, your ability to make connections, collaborate with a team, and think outside the box are the key differentiators in business. Unfortunately, traditional education does not come with a professional handbook. My experience has driven my expertise.

The classroom attempts to provide foundational skills, but there is no textbook that can compete with on-the-job experience. Would an MBA have helped me? Sure. Would I be better equipped to write a business plan had I attended graduate school? Absolutely. (Who are we kidding? I would never have gotten into graduate school!) An MBA is great resume flair, and knowing how to write a business plan has its merits, too, but if you can't get in the room and gain access to the stakeholders, you're nowhere; you're out in the cold, looking in. Call me for a peacoat; I have three.

All the degrees in the world aren't a guarantee for success or happiness (although I'll take one if anyone's handing them out). Social and emotional connections are the catalysts for healthy, lasting relationships—personally and professionally. I believe in a well-rounded education that places equal emphasis on academics and socio-emotional health. Our society places far too much weight on academics alone.

One of my CEO heroes agrees. Sir Richard Branson, high

school dropout and founder of the Virgin Group, says, "Ten years ago, teenagers were being told that university was the be all end all, whereas in reality higher education wasn't of use to many of those paying for it."[3] Branson's a billionaire without a diploma. Go figure.

THE SCHOOL OF LIFE OFFERS THE BEST DEGREE.

3 http://www.theguardian.com/media-network/media-academy-blog/2014/oct/16/richard-branson-too-many-students-were-told-to-go-to-university

"THE PERFECT 7"

Where's the upside in being a "Perfect 10"? There's nowhere to go but down! I prefer being a "Perfect 7." I'm better than average looking and funnier than most, but I am definitely not a 10 —and, look at that—there's room for improvement!

The other night, I asked someone how he would rate himself on a scale of 1-10, and he said he was a 9. I was like, "Are you high? WTF? Seriously, you're not even remotely close to a 9. You're arrogant, you have a comb over, and you're a raging sexist." I even shared my rating system with him, and I still did circles around this guy, minus his Ferrari. He had such a skewed view of himself; he was a 3 tops! I don't even know why I was trying to save him. I told him I'd do three shots of tequila if he shaved his comb over . . . well, he didn't keep his end of the bargain. He was judging himself on money alone, and I had to remind him, "We don't die with the money in our pockets."

My girlfriend always tells me that I'm her #1 best friend. I joke with her and say, "It's way too much pressure! I want to be #2!" I know I'm her #1 friend, but I also know my limitations. I pretty much always forget her birthday, and I rarely show up to her kid's birthday parties. I just want to be who I am: a work in progress! Luckily, she gets it.

You have to be able to look at your flaws and be honest with yourself. They're what make you accessible and genuine. I believe in confidence, but part of that means understanding that no one is great at everything. Come on now! There is always going to be someone prettier, younger, and more dazzling. Ugh! You should see my hot sisters-in-law! My Brothers had to upstage me and marry insanely exotic, smart women.

I've always had flaws —my nose for starters. It's been haunting me for most of my life. I used to face my dates head on in the car so they wouldn't see my profile. (God, they must have thought I was creepy.) In high school, my Stepmother's best friend said to me, "You know, you're cute, but you would be much prettier if you got a nose job." Who says that to a person? I was 16, for fuck's sake! Even so, I've canceled three appointments to get a nose job. What if the famous Beverly Hills plastic surgeon decides to take some creative liberty and I end up with a miniature pug nose? I can't take the risk; I'd rather just play with the cards I was dealt.

In college, my nickname was "Yentl."[4] Oy! I rationalized that stigma to death. That school only had perfect blondes with annoying little perfect symmetrical features. Back then, I was definitely no more than a 5, maybe a 6 on a very good day. I had cystic acne, and I gained way more than the freshman 15—more like the freshman 40. Even though I never finished my last math course, I finished the Nutrisystem program three times! It all adds to your character. Maybe God made me just good-looking enough and threw in a big nose to keep me grounded. It's hard to imagine that somehow I grew into a "Perfect 7!"

---

4 **Yentl** is a 1983 romantic musical drama film from United Artists (through MGM); directed, co-written, co-produced, and starring Barbra Streisand, it was based on the play of the same name by Leah Napolin and Isaac Bashevis Singer, itself based on Singer's short story "Yentl the Yeshiva Boy".

Let's do a little reality check: grade yourself between 1-10 and add up your average totals. Be honest! It will be cathartic to discover you're not perfect. Perfect is BORING!

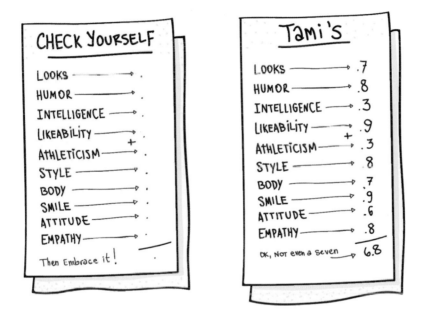

Total Actually, I am at a 6.8. (Close enough!) I can't even get the math to 7.

By the way, I did a facial beauty analysis using the Facial Attractive Index[5] to score my face based on its geometry, and guess what? "A Perfect 7!" It's the nose . . . I told you!

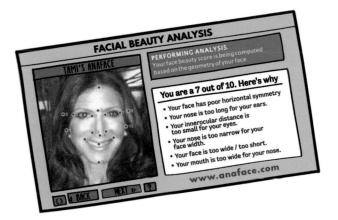

——————— TAMI-ISM ———————
YOU CAN BLAME THE MEN FOR COMING UP WITH A UNIVERSAL SCORING SYSTEM TO RATE PEOPLE'S BEAUTY.

5   See "Hot CEO, Huge IPO" in Chapter 12: *Perception is Reality*, and take your own facial attractiveness assessment at www.anaface.com.

BACKGROUND CHeCK

The last company I ran business development for wound up being acquired by a large consulting firm—we'll just call it Blankety Blank. Prior to the acquisition, we operated like a start-up even though we worked with Fortune 500 clients. It was my job to lead the charge with the C-level relationships, and I was pretty much the Queen of Sheba in that department (if I do say so myself). Well, the new firm had about 360,000 employees, and I wondered how long it would take me to get to know just a few hundred of these new people.

There were some immediate, non-start-up type steps Blankety Blank needed to do to transfer my employment, the first of which was a background check. Okay. This shouldn't be a big deal: no jail time, no drug offenses, all in all I'm a pretty clean chick, not Mary Poppins by any means, but damn close, compared with my friends. Then, it hit me, oh fuck. I had forgotten about that stupid math class from college that I never finished, which meant bingo, no college degree! Ouch. Just admitting that still makes my stomach turn. I had pushed it completely out of my mind! But without a degree, how could Blankety Blank possibly know that I was the shit? (I even won best personality in high school to prove it!) Unfortunately, being irresistibly charming was not part of the background check. I'm not into lying, but if I were, this would have been a fucking fantastic moment to start.

The next day, I got in the car and drove to California State University, Northridge (don't ask) with the full intention of sugar-talking my way into a diploma. No such luck. The department head was out of the office. So, I gathered all of the transcripts from all four of the colleges I had attended, (yes, I attended four colleges and graduated from NONE) and armed myself with paperwork.

When I went to fill out my background check, there was no "other" section where I could explain my circumstances. Where was the blank area to squeeze in the vital information—I had all 257 credits out of 260? I was shit out of luck and shitting in my pants. This meant that, despite my career success, I was going to have to show my hand.

Once all of the paperwork was submitted to the massive HR department, I had to wait a week to hear back. Every minute felt like an hour. I had myself convinced, "no news is bad news." I thought if this whole thing was easy breezy, I would have heard back right away. In those long moments and days, I was thinking it would be better to have a DUI than not to have a diploma. After a week of torture, I found out I passed! (It's a good thing I didn't lie. They would have canned my ass.)

If I were to apply for a job with Blankety Blank today off the street, they would never hire me in a million trillion years. They are a company that values pedigree in education. The best thing that came out of being acquired is now the world assumes I'm uber-intelligent and have an Ivy League degree, because that's the type of person the company recruits and hires. Thanks, Blankety Blank, for making my blank degree more official!

EQ VS. IQ

In the past, our future success was predicted by the highly measurable Intelligence Quotient. The direct correlation between having a high IQ and impressive life accomplishments was undeniable. However, as research, psychology, and the workplace have evolved, studies now show that your Emotional Quotient (or Emotional Intelligence)—which measures your ability to perceive, control, evaluate, and express emotions—has even a stronger impact on your career.

Don't get me wrong—IQ is still a strong determinant of success. Clearly, those who achieve high marks in school tend to continue achieving into their careers. However, when examining those in leadership positions, studies have found that IQ alone is not enough and that, in some areas, it's much less important than EQ.

Article by Keld Jensen in *Forbes* that changed everything for me. In it, he said:

> *Research conducted by the Carnegie Institute of Technology shows 85% of your financial success is due to skills in "human engineering," your personality and the ability to communicate, negotiate and lead. Shockingly, only 15% is due to technical knowledge. Additionally, Nobel Prize winning Israeli-American psychologist, Daniel Kahneman, found, "people would rather do business with a person they like and trust rather than someone they don't, even if the likable person is offering a lower quality product or service at a higher price.*[6]

---

6 (Jensen, 2012) adapted from http://www.forbes.com/sites/keldjensen/2012/04/12/intelligence-is-overrated-what-you-really-need-to-succeed/

Hallelujah! All very good news for us C-students! I was so relieved to find out I didn't have to have the highest IQ in the room to achieve success. To be honest, I had always felt incredibly insecure that I wasn't smart enough to run with the top dogs. It hasn't made life any easier that I've always been attracted to unbelievably intelligent people. You'd think I would be drawn to nincompoops[7], who would make me appear smarter, but no such luck.

I had an associate once who always told me after meetings that I was brilliant in the room. It made no sense to me; in comparison to all of the Ivy Leaguers, I was not brilliant at all. But he never wavered and told me time and time again that I was brilliant, not only because I got us in front of the decision makers, but also because I set the tone that led to the success of the team. His praise made me feel amazing, and it planted the seed of confidence.

For those of you, like me, who didn't learn well in school, have no fear! We high EQ people are finally getting some play. It takes a special person to be able to work a room—to walk in there with confidence and charm the pants off perfect strangers in five minutes. Even more challenging is how well one can think on her feet, turn a negative into a positive, and smooth over an unexpected issue. This is not your subject matter expert, and it's definitely not your technical thinker. This is the talk-your-way-out-of-detention, find-the-loophole, have a fake ID to buy booze for parties (who probably profited from it) person. We have the ability to read the room, know what people need to hear, get on their level, connect with them, and create mutually beneficial business relationships.

7 **Nincompoop:** A person lacking common sense, a person who lacks good sense or judgment / A foolish, stupid or ignorant person.
http://www.urbandictionary.com

Technical savvy can only take you so far. People with high IQs can be so focused on what they're selling that they're not paying attention to what the buyer needs. If you can't talk to people and listen, then you won't have any clients. EQ people understand the relationship comes first. Once the relationship is in place, it's easier to work through issues because both parties are invested emotionally.

A healthy corporate culture is vital to any company's success, and emotional intelligence plays a big role there, too. A recent study by the American Sociological Association found that employers typically hire people they would want to hang out with, and who share similar extracurricular interests. In fact, unsurprisingly, the study also found that employers look for the same personality characteristics in their business candidates as they do in a romantic partner.[8]

According to a CareerBuilder survey conducted by Harris Interactive, "71% of employers value emotional intelligence in an employee more than IQ."[9] When asked why, they replied, employees with high EQ:

* Are more likely to stay calm under pressure;
* Know how to resolve conflict effectively;
* Are empathetic to their team members and react accordingly;
* Lead by example; and
* Tend to make more thoughtful business decisions.

---

8   http://www.asanet.org/documents/press/pdfs/ASR_December2012_Lauren_Rivera_News_Release.pdf

9   http://www.careerbuilder.com/share/aboutus/pressreleasesdetail.aspx?id=pr652&sd=8/18/2011&ed=08/18/2011

Hiring managers felt candidates with high EQ admit and learn from mistakes, can keep their emotions in check in tough situations, listen more than they talk, take criticism well, and show grace under pressure. There's no certification course for that, is there?

STATISTICALLY SPEAKING, WOMEN TEND TO HAVE HIGHER EQ THAN MEN. HA!

THERAPY LESSONS

Just think for a second about how much easier life would be if we learned a few key *life lessons* in the classroom instead of having to figure all of this stuff out on our own! We'd save a shit ton of money, not to mention hours of time on the couch.

Some people think you shouldn't talk about going to therapy, but I disagree. We're all a lifelong work in progress, and there's nothing wrong with admitting you're actively working on yourself. How else are you going to decipher what you might be doing wrong if there is a pattern you should examine, and how you're going to rectify it? What adjustments can you make to fix the shit show? Denial is a popular approach to life and, I'll admit, sometimes I go there. However, the reality is denial is simply a strategy to avoid taking an honest look at yourself. It's also a strategy that will get you nowhere fast.

I've learned some productive, healthy lessons in therapy to help me navigate my environment, many of which translate smoothly from my personal life to business.

For example:

Five in the Hopper: This is a dating tip from one of my therapists (yes, I've had way more than one). To alleviate the pressure of finding the perfect relationship, you should always have five guys in the pipeline and hope to click with one of them. I use the same approach to business: work on five deals; get one of them to sign.

Pie Chart Your Life: Divide your pie into sections that are important to you (work, family, health, relationships, etc.). A healthy scenario is when ¾ of the pie is positive.

Fake It 'Til You Make It: When your confidence is faulty, pretend you've got nerves of steel. If you can talk yourself into believing you're the Queen Bee, you'll feel better. I promise. Sometimes you get knocked down, but you've got to get your game face on, get up, and rise to the occasion.

Feelings: All of your feelings are valid, and we must learn to validate other people's feelings as well as our own. The ability to do this will put out a lot of fires at work and at home.

Fear: Most successful people are worried that they are going to be "found out." Guess what? You ARE capable. You CAN rise to the occasion. Oh, and everyone else is full of shit, too.

It's Not Always About You: People tend to be super responsive to me. I have a weird insecurity when they don't get back to me right away, like I did something wrong, or they're mad at me. Intuitively, I hate conflict, so why the fuck would anyone be mad at me? The point is—it's rarely about you; maybe they are just too busy to return your call?

The Aha Moment: If I applied the skill set I use to build my business relationships to my romantic ones, I would probably be married. (That'll be my next book.)

PRACTICE SELF-AWARENESS.
THE ABILITY TO STAND OUTSIDE YOURSELF
AND LOOK IN IS INVALUABLE FOR PERSONAL
GROWTH AND RELATIONSHIP-BUILDING.

BULLYING IS OUT. BFFING IS IN

When we hear BFF, most people think "Best Friend Forever," but in this book, it's a "Business Friend Forever!" This is not like in middle school when you promise your BFF she'll be the Maid of Honor at your wedding. All of the people you meet and adore can be your Business Friends Forever! I am guessing if they are your BFFs, you are also theirs, and what better way to springboard your friendship into mutual success?

If you travel to work events often like I do, you probably know a lot of people already. However, there are always times when I'm in uncharted territory. No sweat! I look around and think, "Who's going to be my new BFF?" It's like I'm scouting on game day! When I start to unleash my usual, slightly energized, irreverent self, it becomes clear who my BFFs will be based on their reactions. Try to subtract the work component and remember no one wants to talk about work every minute of the day. Everyone wants to let his or her hair down and talk about something else for a change.

One of my favorite BFF connections blossomed over a bad bra choice (mine 😣). I was headed to meet a new client at a conference in Las Vegas wearing what I thought was the perfect outfit: skinny jeans, a white ruffle shirt, a gorgeous tweed jacket, a Gucci belt, and my only pair of Jimmy Choo shoes.

The showroom where we met was like a sauna, and I was sweating from every orifice. I took my jacket off just as the new client was walking over to me. We shook hands, and she gave me the full once-over. While she was looking down at my shirt, she blurted out, "Yeah, that is not working. If you're going to wear a white shirt that is so low cut, you should be wearing a much sexier bra!" I was wearing a plain beige bra. If she only knew how much effort I had put into looking fabulous!

I fumbled through the awkward fashion faux pas and tried to justify my outfit decision. I explained the jacket was supposed to weigh the shirt down so I could lower the buttons. It was meant to be a little sexy, but not too sexy. No one was going to even see the bra, and since it was beige, it would blend in with my skin if there were a slip. Nope. She didn't waiver. At first, I was a bit surprised at her chutzpah[10], but you know what? She was right. I love it; she had the guts to tell me— that's chutzpah!

Months later over cocktails, she confessed she was nervous to meet me and had a foot-in-mouth experience. That's part of why I love her so much because I am a foot-in-mouth kinda girl! She's the real deal! She became my client and even better, my new BFF! And every time I put on my plain Jane beige bra under a white shirt, I think of her.

ALWAYS CARRY
DOUBLE-SIDED TAPE
IN YOUR PURSE ☑

---

10 **Chutzpah** (/ˈhʊtspə/ or /ˈxʊtspə/) is the quality of audacity, for good or for bad. The Yiddish word derives from the Hebrew word ḥutspâ (חֻצְפָּה), meaning "insolence," "cheek," or "audacity." The modern English usage of the word has taken on a broader meaning.
(https://en.wikipedia.org/wiki/Chutzpah)

SORRY, PEOPLE —
IT IS A POPULARITY CONTEST

You've heard the phrase, "it's not what you know, it's who you know," right? Well, it's true. It was a popularity contest in high school, and guess what? It still is! Only now, we get to start over and reinvent ourselves every day.

When I was in high school, this gorgeous new baseball recruit arrived on campus out of the blue. The whole school was buzzing, "Who's the New Guy?" I immediately befriended "New Guy" (the name stuck) by trying to set him up with the prettiest girls. There were so many beautiful girls in our graduating class, and he had a lot to choose from. I was attractive enough, but I didn't even come close to our top 20. Well, guess what??? He liked me, and I became "New Guy's" girlfriend.

At the end of the year, we had to vote for the superlatives (remember those?): best looking, most likely to succeed, best dressed, most popular, best sense of humor, etc. I marched up to my boyfriend and asked, "Did you vote for me for best looking?" In the most definitive voice, he said "Um... NO! I voted for you for best sense of humor." What the fuck? But he was right; I was not the best looking. He was attracted to me for me. I did end up winning best personality, which is a pretty great distinction. He, of course, did win best looking and "the-guy-who-women-want-to-be-stranded-with-on-a-deserted-island" (which was one of the big honors). I have no idea where that dreamy baseball boyfriend is today, but I wonder if his superlatives impacted his career path.

In sales, popularity is an absolute must. The strength of your network and your relationships can make or break your career. This is serious shit.

BE POPULAR FOR THE RIGHT REASONS.

IT'S COOL to Be KiND

How you treat others speaks volumes about your character and, we can all agree, quality people want to work with others who have consistently strong characters. I am often shocked to see how people treat waiters, valets, assistants, or anyone else they deem to be in an inferior position. (When you're nice to the valet, you get VIP parking! Duh.) You have to assume you're being watched and—not to mention, darling—you get more with sugar!! Behaving like an a-hole might work in the short term but it will always come back to bite you (in the a-hole!).

When I was a teenager, I used to work in my Stepfather's law practice as his front desk receptionist. He and I have always gotten along really well. We're two black sheep, which is rare in one family, and he's always offered me comfort as a kindred spirit and fellow wild-child. At one point, he was interviewing to bring in a new associate for the practice. Little did the candidates know, their screening process started the minute they walked in the door. My Stepdad said I was always a good judge of character, and he knew that he could trust me to size someone up for the opportunity.

There was a potential candidate who came into the office, and he was so rude, he turned me off immediately. His whole demeanor was just off and, to make matters worse, he didn't like a piece of art in the lobby and said so. Have you ever? When I went into my Stepfather's office to let him know his interview was there, I put the resume on the desk with a quick thumbs down gesture. That was it; he lost the job before the interview even started.

I thought about this story often when I ventured into my professional life. It was a simple moment in time that carried a deep life lesson: don't see titles, and treat everyone equally. Say hello and thank you to everyone you encounter, because you never know who the gatekeeper is and who is assessing you.

A young rock star associate was telling me a story about how she helped find some untracked money for our department. Without getting too technical, she had access to the system that gave credit to the division that sold a deal. There are occasional circumstances where credit is divided among several departments. Naturally, this creates tension, and there was drama and politics around this one deal. The rock star associate decided to call the lead in the other department and give him full transparency as to why we were fighting for more credit. She said, "I'll be totally honest with you. We are asking for 50% on this deal. For us, it's the difference between making our sales target and not making our target. Can you extend an olive branch and help us out?"

Usually, these guys are sharks, but he said yes! Why? Because he liked this girl: she made him laugh, she was no BS, she was honest, and he wanted to make her look good. She didn't try to use the typical jargon and sweet talk; she just asked politely for a favor and was rewarded in kind.

The interesting thing about this story is that the leader of our department didn't have a strong enough relationship with the head of the other department to ask for a favor. This is how powerful relationships are, regardless of what level you are in the company. It also shows how important gatekeepers are within an organization. Lastly, sometimes we don't even know who the gatekeeper is! Now everyone is kissing her ass, as they should be. As Ellen DeGeneres says at the end of every one of her shows, "Be kind to one another."

I talk about Sir Richard Branson a lot. Why? Because he's awesome! He's a living-breathing testament to practically everything I believe in. A legendary international entrepreneur, he is adamant about treating others with respect. I was lucky enough to be invited to spend a few days with the man himself and about 20 other entrepreneurs on his own private Necker Island. He's everything you'd imagine him to be: charismatic, curious, adventurous, warm, fun, loving, and gorgeous.

During my stay, another guest shared a rumor about a recent visitor to the island who happened to be the owner of a sports team. Apparently, the owner was a bit brash, and Branson himself witnessed him mistreating the staff. His response was swift and final. He simply said, "There will be a boat waiting for you at the dock in 20 minutes to take you to the main island. You are no longer welcome in my home." How cool is he?

> *"Respect is how you treat everyone,*
> *not just those you want to impress."*
> – SIR RICHARD BRANSON

BE NICE TO EVERYONE. YOU NEVER KNOW WHO THE GATEKEEPER IS!

BE A MENSCH[11]

"Shower the people you love with love."
—JAMES TAYLOR

Who doesn't like the feeling of being taken care of? I do! But I'm not the typical executive. I'll take care of you like your favorite aunt or big sister. I may even squeeze your cheeks and bring you home for Passover. I'll hold your hair if you're throwing up (and won't judge you), I'll cut your food, I'll feed you, and I'll nurture the living daylights out of you without even trying.

A mensch is sensitive to others' feelings. When I see insecurities or flaws in others, I don't avoid discomfort; I move towards it and feel their shit with them. People think I'm the Energizer Bunny, but I am not always that person. I have feelings too, you know? I get highs, and with the real highs come real lows. Most of the time, you'll see me laughing and smiling, but I cry, and when I do, I cry hard. You don't want to be around to see that.

When we allow ourselves to be in touch with others, we're more likely to work though the shit it takes to get to the top. Have you ever embarrassed the hell out of yourself when you've had a few too many? Was there someone there to make sure you got home okay? Didn't that feel nice? Be that kind of friend in business.

11   Mensch (*The Joys of Yiddish*), a "mensch" is "someone to admire and emulate, someone of noble character. The key to being 'a real mensch' is nothing less than character, rectitude, dignity, a sense of what is right, responsible, decorous."

BE A CARETAKER
AND SMOTHER THOSE AROUND YOU WITH LOVE.

EVERYONE NEEDS A SHERPA

When I switched careers, I went to an industry event to meet some new people. I must have looked as completely lost as I felt. A wonderful older gentleman approached me and started giving me some advice about how to work the crowd. I welcomed it, because why not? We did a little role reversal, and he gave me a crash course in Networking 101. Reassuringly, he said, "Don't worry, I will be your Sherpa! I've got your back."

Little did I know, this guy was a legend in the business. For years now, we've seen each other at events and stayed in frequent contact. It didn't take my Sherpa long to realize I'm no wallflower and can schmooze with the best of them. He offered to help me as a newbie, and I'm more than willing to help him out whenever he needs it, even though he's doing just fine on his own. These days, we're each other's wingmen, and we share a shtick[12], "This is the first person I met six years ago at an industry event, and he is my Sherpa." He always quips, "And now she is mine!"

A lot of my relationships with clients or associates exist because at one point they were my mentors or I was theirs. It's just a good practice to let other people teach you something. You don't have to play dumb, but I can guarantee you don't know everything there is to know either. If someone wants to give you a leg up, by all means, take it! It's a gift more precious than gold, not to mention they get a

---

12 A **shtick** (Yiddish: קישט) (or **schtick**) is a comic theme or gimmick. "Shtick" is derived from the Yiddish word *shtik* (קיטש), meaning "piece;" the closely related German word *Stück* has the same meaning. The English word "piece" itself is also sometimes used in a similar context. Another variant is "bits of business" or just "bits;" comic mannerisms such as Laurel and Hardy's fiddling with their ties, or one of them looking into the camera shaking his head while the other one would ramble on.

little something out of it too when they see you succeed.

If you're in a new job, find the people you can learn from; people who care about you and your success. The best mentors are those who are willing to lose you as an employee if a better opportunity comes along. They'll be the ones who support what's in your best interests and make sure you are well positioned for whatever's next.

LET OTHERS INVEST IN YOUR SUCCESS.
☆ YOUR MENTORS ARE FOR LIFE. ☆

IT'S MORE FUN WhEnn yOU'RE LAUGHing

"A sense of humor is part of the art of leadership, of getting along with people, of getting things done."
—DWIGHT EISENHOWER

It's crazy how much humor impacts your success at work.[13] If you aren't having fun and laughing, your clients won't be either. There is an art to humor in the workplace. I'm not saying you should necessarily let your inner Joan Rivers (HUGE fan, may she RIP) run wild and offend half the staff. I'm just saying, keep it light. There is a big difference between genuinely having fun vs. being a goofball. Having fun is a reaction to feeling good, being yourself and feeling confident. Being a goofball is Jim Carrey in *Dumb and Dumber.*

If we aren't having fun at work and, as they say, if our work defines us, then how are we perceived by others? Having a good time keeps the attitude positive and increases motivation. Medical science backs me up on this! Smiling and laughing send signals to the brain, which responds by the release of endorphins.

I know that being fun shouldn't be the only reason someone wants to work with you, but the reality is, I've lost business solely because the other people on my team were a drag to be around. Being happy is a choice; it comes from our outlook on life. It's hard to maintain a positive attitude *all* of the time, which, is even more reason to surround yourself with people who know how to find the humor in any situation. Laughter is contagious, so let it fill the room and bring joy to others. Just because you're in a meeting doesn't

---

13 http://www.forbes.com/sites/jacquelynsmith/2013/05/03/10-reasons-why-humor-is-a-key-to-success-at-work/

mean it has to be a snooze fest. Lighten up, Larry!

I was at a marketing summit and sitting in front of a CEO and his client, who was the COO of another firm. I was trying to pay attention to the speaker but was distracted by giggle fits behind me. Something had struck them as funny, and they could not stop laughing. It was the kind of laughing that makes you spit your water out; it can't be contained. The more these grown men tried not to laugh, the harder they were laughing. I was jealous and wanted in on the joke. Everyone did. I still don't have any idea what they were cracking up about, but I look for them every year hoping to find out.

I totally get it! The best chemistry I've ever had was with my female business partner. We started a company that empowered women. We were like sisters and best friends and laughed accordingly. We laughed on the way to the meeting, laughed in the elevator, laughed at the meeting, and laughed all the way to the bank. Being in a room with us was like being on cloud nine! Unfortunately, our momentum came on too fast and quickly ended on the heels of the 2008 crash. I still miss our giggle fits and the high our chemistry created; we had fun while it lasted!

What's more fun than doing business with your buddies?

"The most wasted of all days is one without laughing."
—E.E. CUMMINGS

LAUGHING IS PRODUCTIVE.

KEEP it SIMPLE

"If you can't explain it simply,
you don't understand it well enough."
—ALBERT EINSTEIN

Always explain your product or capabilities in the simplest way possible. Fight the urge to impress your audience with a bunch of technical gobbledygook. Break down your offering as you would for a child. Pretend they know nothing. Talk to them like a fourth grader.

We are responsible for educating clients so they can make an informed decision. How do you test a child on what they know? You make them explain it to you. The best ideas and solutions are those that can be explained easily to any audience. If you're confident your audience can do the same for the other stakeholders in their organization, you've done your job. If not, you need to evaluate why not. Chances are your presentation needs to be simplified.

"I'm not grammatical in the way I talk, or in the way I
write, and I don't pretend to be. I'm a high school dropout who
eavesdrops."
—JACKIE COLLINS

I love learning from people, but I promise, it has nothing to do with big vocabulary. Actually, I find fancy words off-putting, especially when the word choice seems pretentious and elicits the "the smarty pants effect." I want to ask, "Are you trying to let us know you're smarter than we are?" I'm not one of those people who will just nod like I know what they're talking about. I'll either ask what the word means or Google it. Then I'll wonder why the fuck they didn't just simplify it, and I'm probably not the only one.

Assess the audience and communicate your message based on the lowest common denominator. This skill will quickly make you the go-to person for all of the answers.

A Princeton research paper, "Consequences of Erudite Vernacular Utilized Irrespective of Necessity: Problems with Using Long Words Needlessly" by Daniel M. Oppenheimer,[14] proves that big words can make you look dumb.

Oppenheimer's study performed three experiments. He tested college essays, foreign language papers, and even a research paper, and the results were unanimous. In each case, the simpler version scored a much higher rating. So, there you have it—from Princeton, no less! Real life is not the vocabulary section of the SATs. Speak clearly, in a language we can all understand, and you'll be amazed at the response you get.

Smarty Pants (vs) Tami Pants!

Convivial ——————⟿ Fun
Efficacious ——— ⟿ Successful
Cogent ——————⟿ Persuasive
Affable ——————⟿ Likeable

The same goes for client presentations. An excellent way to keep a presentation simple is to practice your summary. I come from the entertainment business where I sold TV shows and film ideas. I learned the most successful pitches include a logline, which is an art

---

14 http://www.ucd.ie/artspgs/semantics/ConsequencesErudite.pdf

form in and of itself. Essentially, it's the ability to excite and intrigue the buyer through a brief summary. Save them the hassle of having to read 120+ pages of script. In regular business-speak, it's referred as an "elevator pitch." Call it whatever you want, but the question is: Can you explain your objective or idea in once sentence?

* **Movie Example**—*The Hangover* logline: A Las Vegas-set comedy centered around three groomsmen who lose their about-to-be-wed buddy during their drunken misadventures, then must retrace their steps to find him.

* **Business Example**—*Rent the Runway* logline: An online rental service for women who want to look fabulous and wear designer dresses for a fraction of the cost.

BE ACCESSIBLE. KEEP IT SIMPLE.

KNOW A LITTLE ABOUT A LOT
(TMZ, ESPN, AND CNN ShOULD COVER it)

You have to have something to talk about when you walk into a room. If the gift of gab doesn't come quickly for you, research the shit out of the people you're meeting with. Insight into their past work experience, hobbies, interests, family, political views, dance moves ☺ —you name it—it's at your fingertips, so start stalking. No, you're not a crazy person; you're getting to know your audience so you can easily find a common ground and break the ice.

Knowledge is power. There's no need to force it, but if you can subtly and organically incorporate a few of the nuggets you've uncovered, people will respond favorably. And please, be cool. Don't start listing all the things you know about the person, because that's just creepy. It's always best to come across as generally inquisitive, even if you know every friggin' detail about their undergrad at Columbia and their MBA at Wharton. Shoot for a casual, "You went to school in New York, right? Was it NYU?" Catch my drift? Not to mention, people love talking about themselves, so if you tell them everything you know— you're screwed.

Education and general background information are a great start, but if you've done your homework, you should have a solid idea of the person's interests and passions. If those aren't in line with your own, give yourself a crash course: TMZ, CNN, and ESPN should give you everything you need! You don't have to be a genius expert specialist on the topic; an overall sense is sufficient.

Being a generalist translates to the ability to shoot the shit about many topics. According to Bill Wagner, from Entreprenuer.com, "Generalists are strategic thinkers. They are big picture-oriented, prefer environments where they can use their results-driven nature, enjoy autonomy and independence, and are stronger risk-takers."[15]

If you use this tactic strategically, you'll find people are flattered that you know a little about them. I spend more time briefing my team on the personality types and backgrounds of execs we're meeting with than I do on what the company's needs are. Let them tell you what they need; that's the easy part. Your goal should be to find out who they are as people. Remember, you're looking for that connection point. Use pop culture to bridge the gap until you can get them to spill the beans on something personal.

PREPARATION IS ESSENTIAL.
DON'T WALK INTO THE ROOM
LOOKING LIKE A NINCOMPOOP.

---

15 http://www.entrepreneur.com/article/84134

THE ART OF LISTENING

"A conversation is a dialogue, not a monologue."
—TRUMAN CAPOTE

God only knows, this is an area I've had to work on big time, especially with my "A+" skills in talking too much. In meetings, you must practice listening 75% of the time and talking the other 25%. When you're talking the whole time, you're in a one-way conversation with yourself, and there is no room to collaborate. Go into the room as if you are forming a partnership (because you are!), have a conversation, and build the relationship. If you go into a meeting with the strategy to pitch, pitch, and pitch, then you won't have time to understand the client's needs and it will seem as if you're only interested in solving your own problems. We want our clients to look good, and we want to solve *their* problems. Our goal is to make their lives easier and, to do so, we've got to give them the floor.

Listening is important; listening *in person* is vital. Are you just hearing or are you listening with every sense available? Nodding, smiling, and other physical reactions indicate active listening. Look for social cues and pay attention to body language, tone, and mannerisms. Are they hiding something or are they revealing something? Turn on your inner Sherlock Holmes.

We've all made the common mistake of overcompensating by talking too much in an attempt to cover every base. Rambling on and on gives the impression you are:

- ☐ Nervous
- ☐ Unsure of your product
- ☐ Ill-prepared
- ☐ Unconcerned with the client's needs
- ☐ Desperate (gross)
- ☑ All of the above

Your goal is to give the client what they want and, usually if you listen and pay attention, they'll tell you what that is. So stop selling and if you do need to speak, ask clear questions about their goals, objectives, and desired outcomes. Just keep them talking. The more people brain dump, the more they'll open up, and the more insight you'll have. And just think, they did all the work!

SHUT UP AND LISTEN
TO THE CLIENTS' NEEDS.
PUT ELECTRICAL TAPE ON YOUR MOUTH,
IF YOU MUST.

GIVE A SHIT AND GIVE BACK

Not only does charitable activity help others and make you feel good about yourself, but it also gives you something interesting to talk about! You'll be amazed at the connections you'll make when you find like-minded people who share your passions.

Give a shit about something other than yourself and, by default, you'll be in an elite class of influential people. The charitable set offers a nice change of scenery and the opportunity to interact with people from various backgrounds. You aren't there to compete for business, and you have an easy icebreaker: who connected you to this cause? Have you been affected personally? It's more rewarding to be part of a small group of people who share your goals and mindset than a large group only concerned with personal gain or an agenda. Contribute to a charity; I promise you'll meet people who will inspire and rejuvenate you in all areas of your life.

When I have free time, I volunteer, which feels much better than just writing a check. But, if you're busy—write some checks and skip the extra glass of wine at happy hour! Helping the people around you is worth every penny and may cut calories. Even if you're broke, you can find $10 somewhere. Whether you have emotional support to lend, your time, or your dollars (credit cards, PayPal, and bitcoins work too), a good karma bank returns lifetime rewards, and generosity knows no price tag. Heaven or hell—you choose!

I have a sponsored daughter in Cambodia through CCF[16] and I recently went to visit her. The trip changed my life in ways that

---

16 Children's Cambodia Fund: https://www.cambodianchildrensfund.org

are hard to express. Meeting her and seeing how she and her family live put everything into perspective. I have been able to impact the quality of her life, but it's really how she has changed mine that is so amazing.

My friends say, "What you are doing for this little girl is so great," but I don't see it that way. Whenever my own life or work seems tough, I picture her, so full of joy and optimism despite having so little and experiencing unimaginable atrocities, and my mindset changes instantly. The challenges I face are nothing in comparison. Her attitude and spirit has shifted mine in a new way. We really have no idea what it's like to live on a garbage dump. Insert Jewish (or religion of choice) guilt here. What do you have to lose? You might even save money in the long run by passing on that pair of Louboutins. Go feed 100 children instead.

GET INVOLVED IN SOMETHING BIGGER THAN YOURSELF.
THE REWARDS ARE BIGGER THAN YOUR PAYCHECK,
AND YOU NEVER KNOW WHAT MUCKETY-MUCK
MIGHT BE INVOLVED, TOO.

BUSINESS IS LIKE DATING

It's easy to get caught up in sales strategies, pitch tactics, networking game plans, and all of the other bullshit you do to get business. Take a step back. Look at it from a different perspective. Approach it the exact same way you would dating. Business relationships aren't much different from personal relationships. Think about it; it's the same song and dance, the same wooing process, and the same razzle-dazzle—look at me, I'm the hottest! Pick me! Pick me! And just like dating, if they think you're interested in someone else (i.e., a competitor), they'll want to take you off the market altogether.

It's imperative to get to know your clients as people, including their quirks and habits, if you want to maintain a trusting and honest relationship. If you don't lay the groundwork, your clients won't stick around when a competitor tries to sweep them off their feet. You need to nurture the relationship and keep the romance alive, and don't forget about your regular clients while you're out courting new ones! Whenever you question your approach, ask yourself, "What would I do if I were dating (or trying to date) this person?"

CLOSING THE DEAL IS THE SAME
PROCESS AT WORK AS IT IS AT HOME.
BUT WHEN YOU'RE AT WORK,
KEEP IT CLEAN!

Dating Behavior   vs   Business Behavior

Dating Behavior	Business Behavior
The Attraction	Recognizing the $$$ opportunity
Getting up the nerve to approach	The Introduction
Compliments / Flirting	Buttering up the client
Getting him/her to laugh	Building a connection
Asking him/her out	Securing the meeting
The Game	Beating the competition
Dating Period	Collaborating and foundation building
Closing the Deal	Securing the client
Getting Married	Signing a multi-year deal

-Translate as you please-

KNOW HOW TO THROW A PARTY

An associate and I were reminiscing about a party we (accidentally) threw a couple of years ago at a fancy ski resort. My CEO had booked the penthouse suite for this hip conference we were attending—but he didn't show up!

In the interest of saving face (and having a good time), I felt an obligation to host a party in this fabulous space. I didn't even know who was attending the conference until I arrived, but when I saw the list I thought, "WTF? I'll just invite every executive on the list. Who doesn't want to go to a party in the penthouse?"

I was staying there with two men—one was my favorite associate, and the other was a Wall Street guy who was doing some business with my CEO. On the day of the party, the guys called and asked if I needed them to pick up any supplies. Pleasantly surprised by their chivalry, I gave them a specific, itemized list of simple appetizer-type food, champagne, etc.

What did they show up with? A couple of cases of cheap beer, red plastic Solo cups (as if this was a kegger!), and a bunch of assorted potato chips. Oy! Boys! Don't get me wrong, I have a deep appreciation for both potato chips and keggers, but are you kidding me? We were supposed to be professional adults, inviting C-level guests to our luxury penthouse, on behalf of our CEO, in the hope of getting millions of dollars worth of business. I buried the potato chips in the closet along with the Solo cups.

This required an emergency trip to the liquor store. I loaded up on Yellow Label Veuve Clicquot and top-shelf booze to stock the bar. Room service delivered cheese platters, crudité, and the appropriate glassware. It was coming together like magic. I was on a roll. If you're in my home (or penthouse), you'll be treated like the VIP you are!

The party was a huge hit, and the guys learned a thing or two about how to throw it all together, with limited prep time, and without it looking like a fraternity bash. I trained them well and it turns out, they made great hosts after all!

YOUR PARTIES ARE A DIRECT REFLECTION
OF WHO YOU ARE AND HOW YOU DO BUSINESS.
TAKE IT UP A NOTCH.

DON'T TAKE "NO" FOR AN ANSWER

I don't take no for an answer because I am a YES girl (more on that later). My business partners and I were shopping a reality TV show about the MIT crew that brought down Las Vegas. The premise was fantastic, but we needed to get the casino group to buy-in before we could pitch it to TV networks with confidence. After some finagling, I finally got a meeting with the head of entertainment at Caesar's Casino. This was huge; it would make or break the show.

We prepared every day and, at the very last minute, the Caesar's executive called to cancel. My kneejerk reaction was, "NO!!!!!" which is exactly what I blurted out. It was a bold move, but I had to commit to it. "I'm already here in Las Vegas, and I'm sorry, but canceling is not an option." He was taken aback; but, hey, we shouldn't have to suffer because he overbooked his schedule. After he felt my hands grab him by the throat through the phone, he agreed to 15 minutes.

Well, that 15 minutes turned into eight hours. We combined the rest of our meetings, grabbed some drinks, went out to dinner, and hit up a nightclub afterward. I even taught him how to work his own VIP status at the club. That was eight years ago. Since then, he's been on the board of one of my companies and become one of my best friends. I even attended his son's bris[17] (which is a Jewish ritual, a ceremonial circumcision . . . a little snippety snip, intimate friends and family only).

I was trained to be hungry and go after what I want; starving is

17   **Bris:** The rite or ceremony of male circumcision, usually performed on the eighth day of life. (Hebrew:בְּ הלָימְ תירְ,),pronounced[bʁit miʾla]. (http://dictionary.reference.com/browse/bris)

not an option. As an entrepreneur, you cannot base actions on fear. Is there any such thing as "No, we can't work together"? No! Everything is relationship-driven. If you have a solid relationship, you'll find a way to work together. This doesn't mean I'm blowing off an opportunity or that I'm aloof (or that I take "No" for an answer). On the contrary—it's a positive focused energy. It's the awareness we must adopt in order to succeed, centered in confidence and drive. If we are not working together now, I know we will eventually.

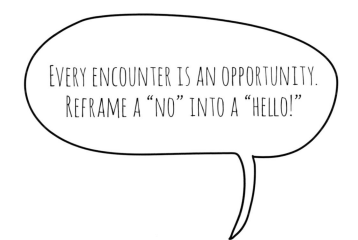

ASK FOR THE BUSINESS

Walk in that door assuming you have the business on lockdown. This is not a license to be cocky or ill-prepared, but it will calm your nerves and give off positive energy, which has a domino effect in the boardroom. When you believe in yourself and think you are the best choice for the client, you send a clear signal that they should believe in you, too. The power of persuasion works, but you need to *ask for the business*.

When the time comes, read the room and assess the situation. If the client appears wishy-washy or if the relationship is new, introduce a pilot project as a "proof of concept," which is a safe way to get your feet wet with each other. It might not be the right time to go for the whole enchilada, maybe they just want to try the guacamole —like dating, if they like it, they can put a ring on it. Asking for a million dollars might seem like a lot, but it could be a drop in the bucket for an even bigger contract down the road. How're you gonna get it if you don't ask?

When the meeting is over, instead of promising follow-up materials, let them know how excited you are to work together. Never deviate from this declarative: we *will* work together. Keep the ask high energy and fun and let them know they can expect more of the same when you're working together.

My associates laugh when I do this, but it works! They say, "You ask for millions of dollars, and then giggle like it's no big deal!" I love getting in the room and bringing in the business, but there is an end game here. If I've done the work to score the meeting, do you think I'm going to shy away from the big ask? Hell no.

 NEVER LEAVE A MEETING
WITHOUT MAKING YOUR ASK.

THE ULTIMATE TIEBREAKER: YOUR TEAM

In business, there is always going to be a need to differentiate your-self from the competition—a concept that will be drilled into you, if it hasn't been already. Finding that edge can be difficult at times. If you have similar value propositions, there are the obvious avenues to try for a leg up:

★ We are the more cost efficient option;
✴ We offer better terms and flexibility; and
★ Our benefits outshine anyone else's.

However, the strongest ace in the hole, "I will trump my com-petition" every single time, guaranteed differentiator is a fucking fantastic team. The first thing I do when selling to anyone is talk up the great people that surround me. My associates are like fam-ily and I treat (and tout) them as such. They're the A-team and I'd be up the creek without a paddle if I didn't have a core group of people I can count on to deliver what I'm selling.

Your clients have a choice who they do business with, and I assure you, they will pick great people over product any day of the week. Keep this in mind when you're selecting your team. One bad apple really can spoil the barrel, so don't throw some schmuck into the mix just because you need extra bodies. One negative is the equivalent of five positives, so get rid of that whole "strength in numbers" BS. The strength lies with the individuals who work well together. Ask yourself: who will the client respond to and have chemistry with?

I am careful to highlight the commonalities between the asso-ciates and the clients. Maybe they both play golf, or they're both from New Jersey, or they're both mad about the Lakers, etc. As such, I've laid the groundwork for an emotional connection before they even talk to each other. It's the same principle of teeing up a sale, but in this case, I'm teeing up the team. These are the people who are going to drive it home and make us all look good.

YOU'RE ONLY AS STRONG AS THE PEOPLE AROUND YOU.

BE PRESENT. AKA PUT YOUR FUCKING PHONE AWAY

Being present in both mind and body is a challenge—fewer and fewer people can drown out distractions and be truly present in their environment. While advances in technology have made us all more accessible and efficient, they have also created barriers. We're more connected than ever, in the most disconnected of ways. I can assure you, there is nothing more powerful than sitting in front of someone, live (not via satellite or Skype) in a room. There is no text message, email, or ping equivalent to a face-to-face conversation. Regardless of your work environment or industry, your clients need to know that you are 100% focused and engaged with them.

How much do you think you miss on a daily basis because your head is buried in your phone as you walk down the street? Sometimes my most significant contacts come from a seemingly insignificant nod, or a brief hello in an elevator, or a glance in a hallway. Contrary to popular belief, multi-tasking does not make you more efficient because you aren't giving any one thing or one person your undivided attention. We have become conditioned to check our device every two seconds, but be mindful of what message this activity sends to others. If you're hunched over your phone tapping away, does this make you approachable to others?

Being fully engaged is contagious. If you're present in the moment with someone—having dinner, drinks, coffee, one-on-one conversation—do you think they will be checking their phone or looking around if you're not? Set the precedent.

 BE PRESENT WHEN YOU ARE PHYSICALLY PRESENT—AS IN YOU CAN PINCH ME.

THE IMPORTANCE OF BODY LANGUAGE

Public perception is directly linked to physical movement. There's a reason they call it "body language." You're communicating without words, but are you conveying the right message? Do you appear standoffish and disconnected? Or are you inviting and open? I'm not talking about Sharon Stone in *Basic Instinct* "open," you don't want to send that message, but you should avoid crossing your arms over your chest and rocking a bitchy resting face.

The best way to strengthen your self-awareness is through observation. Look around the room. Do you notice anyone looking down or otherwise avoiding eye contact? What kind of signal are they sending? Eye contact is one of the most vital forms of communication. When someone isn't making eye contact, they come off as disengaged, distracted, bored, or insincere. Basically, like they don't give a fuck. My eye contact advice? Abide by the European rule of toasting—make eye contact with everyone. The superstition in France is if you fail to do this, you are destined to have bad sex for seven years. So, if you're feeling anti-social at the company mixer, remember that a considerable portion of your sex life hangs in the balance! Mingle. Talk. Observe. Move about the room with purpose.

They say taking up space shows power. Well, if that's the case, I am one powerful woman. I'm tall, I have the longest monkey arms on the planet, and I'm kinesthetically inclined, if you will. I talk with my hands. Always. Someone once challenged me to try to talk without using my hands. Total fail. I sat on my hands but couldn't adequately express myself using just words. No matter where I am—even if I'm alone on the phone—I'm using my hands. I'm well aware I look like a total fucking idiot (think if Molly Shannon in *Superstar* had a baby with Olive Oyl from *Popeye*) flailing my arms all around, but hey, it's me. I am lanky, uncoordinated, and I might come off as a bit crazy if you're observing my conversation from a safe distance. I'm likely waving, laughing, hugging—you name it. The physicality may come off as slapstick comedy, but come on, who wouldn't want to hang out with that? Total power play.

BEWARE OF THE NON-VERBAL SIGNALS YOU ARE SENDING.

TAMESE: ENTHUSIASM IS CONTAGIOUS

Just as your body sends messages, so does the intonation of your voice. Have you ever noticed when some people speak, they don't change their tone, and you get lost in a sea of words and information? Your eyes start to glaze over, and your brain goes numb. Then, someone else speaks and suddenly you snap back to attention. What happened? They may be talking about the same thing, but somehow, this new person is more engaging. Well, that's me! This language has a name—Tamese. When I'm speaking Tamese, I'm so passionate, I'm talking a million miles a minute (arms flailing wildly all the while) and the point is, it's contagious, and people buy into my enthusiasm.

I had an associate once who looked exactly like Tom Brady. Whenever he walked into the room, men, women, and anyone with a pulse were like, "Oh HELLO." He had beauty and brains, and everyone had a business crush on him, but then he opened his mouth. His voice had no intonation, and it just went on and on. His monotone pitch got zero response, so he would launch into that overcompensating thing we all do when we're not getting the desired reaction. Listening to him talk was like watching paint dry while under sedation. When we had pitch calls, and he took the lead, I would literally put him on speaker and clean my whole house while he droned on endlessly.

The intonation is the rise and fall of someone's voice. Think of it as the melody or music of language. It conveys confidence (or lack thereof) and adds drama to keep things exciting. Speech scientists say the intonation of a sentence provides us with 70% of its meaning.[18] It doesn't matter how you look, or even what you're saying; it's *how you say it* that either gets people hooked or makes them want to give YOU the hook.

IF YOU WANT TO KEEP YOUR AUDIENCE ENGAGED, BE ENTHUSIASTIC WHEN SPEAKING!

18   http://accentonbusiness.net/intonation-speaks-volumes/

COLLABORATING VS. PITCHING

Collaboration: Working with others to do a task and achieve shared goals.

Pitching: A planned presentation of a product or service designed to initiate and close a sale.

The difference between these two terms is significant. We'll get into the many nuances of a pitch (and even talk about the No-pitch pitch strategy) a little later on, but as a general rule, try to approach every meeting and interaction with collaboration in mind. Avoid asking to "present your capabilities" whenever possible.

My intention is to promote partnership over a seller/customer relationship. My follow-ups always inquire as to when we can work together again and an invitation to compare notes. This is an inclusive and equalizing approach versus a hard sell.

The relationship should be about what the client needs, not what you want to sell them. It's like serving crab and lobster because you think it's decadent and, therefore, desirable. But has anyone stopped to ask the client about food allergies? Show them their interests and tastes are top of mind and serve them what they want!

 INCLUDE THE BUYER IN THE PROCESS.

MEETINGS TO GET MEETINGS

Certain business behaviors have been ingrained into corporate culture just from sheer habit. What is it with the fixation on meetings? I get the importance of landing the "big one" or strategizing with your team in advance, but more times than I can count, I've seen meetings scheduled on the topic of "how to get a meeting" or worse, "the agenda for the meeting." Do we really need a task force of 30 some people, all of whom make a minimum of $200K a year, to strategize about how to get a single meeting, or what to talk about in the meeting? It's laugh-out-loud funny.

Meetings tend to multiply like rabbits. The first meeting turns into months of action plans, follow-up items, and calendar invitations to more meetings—all centered around how to get one meeting with one person. When I think of how much money and time is wasted, it makes me a little crazy. But then again, it also reinforces how much value I bring because I already know how to get into the friggin' room!

Hey guys, I don't mean to speak out of turn, but I have an idea. See that rectangular device that almost never leaves your hand and is with you at all times? It's called a phone. Dial the number and call the person you want to meet with! Or, plan B, find out where they are going and meet them there. Have your CEO email their CEO. Find a friend of a friend via social media and get an intro, but for the love of God, stop planning meetings to get meetings.

 TAKE SOME INITIATIVE AND LINE UP A MEETING ALREADY!

SHIT HAPPENS

In business, as in life, rarely does everything go exactly as planned. Quite the opposite. Clients often say, "How can we prevent something from going wrong?" Let's face reality. Usually, there are several people involved, often from different teams with varying roles. The potential for error exists. So, I always answer the question honestly. "I can assure you, something will get screwed up."

That being said, start by anticipating potential issues with the client. Full disclosure and showing you have nothing to hide earns trust upfront. Then, walk them through how quickly the potential issues can be resolved and what impact (minimal) these questions may have on the project. In my experience, problems arise as a result of a breakdown in communication. Since I don't usually control the whole process, the key is to identify that breakdown, fix the issue, and develop an action plan to prevent it from happening again.

I want to promise my clients perfection (because, fuck, I'm in sales), but since I can't predict the future or control human error, I can only instill confidence in my ability to fix the shit until we are back to our happy place and hit the local bar.

NEVER PROMISE PERFECTION.

THE RESUME

Resume. What an ugly word. We should follow the Brit's lead on this and just call it a CV (curriculum vitae); it sounds so much cooler. Resume = desperate for a job.

Any time I've considered a pivot in my career, my first thought is always inevitably, "Ugh. Shit. Resume? Really?" Although I've rarely needed one, updating that fucker is such a dreadful undertaking, isn't it? You open up your last version praying it has *some* relevant information about your current role, which it almost never does. When you finally build up the motivation to sit down and work on it, you're faced with the frustrating task of trying to describe what the fuck it is you do all day. I can't even explain to my parents what I do all day. How am I going to get this down on paper?

You're all over that thesaurus like white on rice to come up with the most impressive adjectives that make you sound important without misrepresenting your experience. How do you gloat appropriately about your home runs without sounding like a douche? Most of what I do can't be boiled down to a bullet point!

How do you apply a mathematical equation to your accomplishments? (We all know those recruiters love goddamn stats.) It simply doesn't work to use math (remember, I didn't graduate from college because I failed math) to demonstrate measurable gains in my current position. If I tried, it would read: "Tami's rate of return is 85% with existing clients if attending a two-day conference." Or, "Tami has enhanced our business in the last year by 26% based on her ability to throw a good party people actually want to attend."

As we know, I can't fall back on my spectacular educational accomplishments, either. My grade point average was "Negative 4.0 Magna Cum Laude." Once in a while, I did get a good grade, but only because the teacher liked me and wanted me to succeed. Because of my likeability I got a "B" in college Spanish and the only thing I can say in my best valley girl accent, is "¿Hola, que tal? Muchas gracias. No bueno. Nada mas." (P.S. My loss, I wish I knew Spanish.) In other words, my font choice better be pretty dazzling.

I've accepted that my skills and experience can't be demonstrated in a resume format with specific time frames, and textbook methodologies applied to real-life. It's like describing snow to someone who has never left Bora Bora—no matter how many adjectives and comparisons I use, they just need to experience Antarctica during a blizzard to fully understand. Naturally, this creates a bit of a hiccup for both my potential employer and me. Since I can't adequately explain myself on paper, I must be my own CV, live in the flesh!

WHAT YOUR RESUME SAYS YOU DO	TRANSLATION
Prioritizes workload efficiently to complete projects under strict timelines.	I'm doing the job of two people and put out the most important fires first so we don't lose the business.
Easily adaptable and takes initiative in an evolving industry.	Shit is inconsistent, and we have zero guidance or direction, so I wing it and hope for the best.
Collaborates and liaises across multiple teams, enhancing strategic partnerships within departments to increase client satisfaction.	None of these fucks get along with each other, which makes us inefficient. So while they internally measuring dick size, I ignore it and put the client first.
Anticipates areas of growth and communicate this to leadership in order to exceed firm targets.	I figure out how to make even more money for the company, and then tell my boss how to do it and watch him or her take all of the credit (which is fine if I am getting my commission).

The good news is, recent studies have shown that online presence is going to replace your resume by 2020. According to Forbes.com, there are a number of reasons to put more focus on your social media accounts than your one-to-two page life summary.[19] In short, here's why:

★ People message more frequently through social media channels, and less through email;

✳ Forbes.com writer Susan Adams shared a webjob.com survey reporting only 23% of jobseekers found jobs through ads. Employers find you;

★ Resumes are dated. All of the online tools have taken the individuality out of them. Employers prefer to look at your LinkedIn account and Facebook page to assess both professional acumen and how you will fit into the corporate culture; and

★ My favorite. The entrepreneurial mindset: there is a new professional in town, the kind who manages his or her career like entrepreneurs, always on the grind, scouting new opportunities to cash in. Scott Gerber, author of *Never Get a Real Job*, says, "You need to create a job to keep a job."

My twin Brother is an example of the last point. He cold-called the CEO of his company and convinced him that they were leaving money on the table, and persuaded them to hire him.

Your under-two-page resume is not the sole tool (or even the most effective tool) at your disposal when seeking your next career move. You have countless avenues to share your goals, accom-

---

19 http://www.forbes.com/sites/danschawbel/2011/02/21/5-reasons-why-your-online-presence-will-replace-your-resume-in-10-years/

plishments, opinions, interests, passions, creativity and experience with the world.

According to *Business Insider*, "After years of looking at the data, Google has found that things like college GPAs and transcripts are almost worthless in hiring. Following these revelations, the company is hiring more and more people who never even went to college."[20] Halle-fucking-lujah!

BE CREATIVE IN HOW YOU PRESENT YOURSELF TO POTENTIAL EMPLOYERS TO STAND OUT FROM THE PACK.

---

20 http://www.businessinsider.com/google-hiring-non-graduates-2013-6

CHAPTER 4

NO MEETING NO CHOOS

GO TO FIRST BASE

For God's sake, if you have talked to these people on the phone or had any prior introduction, give them a hug and kiss hello! Just open your arms and pucker up those lips (but no tongue!). Don't treat them like strangers. This creates an energy shift in the room; you've already found a way to break the ice, and you're doing it with affection.

Countless times I've walked into a meeting and was the only person from my team who greeted the client with any familiarity or indication we'd met before. Occasionally an associate is uncomfortable with my friendly ways, but I don't care! Sometimes, they'll try to make excuses for me as if I'm doing something wrong and say, "I know, she's a hugger" and kind of roll their eyes. In return, I want to make excuses for them and say, "I know, they're just so fucking uptight, but I promise they have a high IQ!" I get it; not everyone is a hugger, but more often than not, people respond favorably. Take a chance; show some love.

Many years ago, I worked briefly with my twin Brother as a strategic partnership consultant for his media company. We were meeting with the head of development for a TV show at a big-time studio. I walked right in and gave the top executive a hug. On the way out, I gave her another hug and a kiss on the cheek. In the elevator, my Brother said, "Have you two met before?" I said, "No, but I spoke to her on the phone." He said (weirded out), "It's kind of strange that you hug and kiss everyone." I was a little bummed out because isn't it just the worst feeling when you're criticized by your own family?

Naturally, I started to question this aspect of my personality, but not for long! Fast forward to a month later at the follow-up meeting. The executive greeted both of us with open arms and showed serious interest in moving forward with the project. Back in the elevator, my Brother said, "Remember when I questioned why you hug and kiss everyone? Yeah, I was wrong. Keep doing it, it works!"

I have to admit; it's fun to catch people off guard with outward displays of affection. Sometimes, they look at me like I'm a freak, but I'm having fun on the inside, and it always breaks down their walls.

You have to read the room. If it absolutely does not feel right, err on the side of caution and give them a damn firm handshake. I've misread the social cues and gone in for the hugs and kisses and felt like a dork; it happens. Practice makes perfect!

The emotional connection shifts to a deeper level of intimacy when you have some kind of physical contact with someone. Plus, it's much harder to say no to someone when you've already gone to first base.

WHEN YOU'RE WOOED

When I was at my last job, a competitor called to woo me over to his company. That's always a good feeling because it means people are talking about you in a good way! Although I was happy where I was, I indulged him in the poaching attempt. We talked about his business model, goals, needs, etc. Just as we were about to get off the phone, I gave him the Tami test. I said, "You know, I don't execute. I don't even know your industry. The ONLY thing I do is build high-level relationships." He said, "Tami, I can bring anyone in to execute and any number of experts in the field, but no one can get in the goddamn room!"

GOOD BUSINESS DEVELOPMENT EXECUTIVES ARE RARE.

JEWISH PERSUASION

Guilt is a magical yet lethal power, and since I've been the recipient of the guilt treatment, I know it's like playing with fire. Nevertheless, I've been well-trained in guilt, like a top gun, by my Jewish mother, and when necessary, it's my Hail Mary to go in for the kill in business.

After setting up a series of meetings with a major brand to discuss new business opportunities, I flew to New York with my whole team and our new boss. I was pretty good friends with one of the top executives, who tried to cancel the meeting at the last minute with a really lame excuse. No way José! Did I mention my new boss was along? This meeting was not getting derailed. It was my time to shine! I ended up kicking my Hail Mary play into high gear. A couple of text messages and a hard-core, guilt-filled voicemail later, the executive changed his tune, and was ready to meet, and drove back to his office. Our one-hour meeting turned into three-plus and dinner afterward. Jewish persuasion is a highly effective method of getting what you want. Just ask my Mom.

USE WHATEVER IT TAKES
TO GET IN THE ROOM.

START WITH YES

One of the reasons I've had success securing meetings can be summed up in one word: YES. We are trained at an early age to be skeptics, anticipate problems, and consider risks. My niece, who is five, and nephew, three, usually give me a resounding, "NO!" before I even finish my question. I'll ask, "Do you want a dollar?" NO. "Do you want a 100 dollars?" NO. "Do you want 1,000 dollars?" NO. I don't know what world they're living in; those kids are crazy!

Find the Yes people; the ones who are up for a challenge and willing to take a calculated risk. When I worked in the entertainment industry, it was a lot easier to sell a show if there was a seasoned, successful writer attached to it, as opposed to a talented, but less-established writer—even if the latter was better. I found a way to work around the challenge by seeking out the Yes people. Typically, they're much more fun, anyway. Yes has risks, but the rewards are sweeter.

There have been numerous times when I've said, "No, I can't." Nine times out of ten that response was driven by fear. It's easier to say no and play it safe, but over time, I realized missing an opportunity is more painful than failing in the moment. Failure is inevitable, but it's also a necessary precursor to success. Change your auto-responder to Yes and surround yourself with others who speak the same language.

"YES" OPENS DOORS.

CHUTZPAH[21]

If you want to land the business, you gotta show 'em what you're made of. This is no time for pussyfooting[22] around. It took me a year, but I finally landed a meeting with a hotshot executive from one of the largest consumer product companies of a super hip brand. This wasn't just any executive, either; he was a baller.[23]

Shortly before the scheduled dinner in Chicago, he tried to back out, citing time constraints. Knowing it was impossible, he told us he could only go if we moved the reservation to 7 p.m. and he named an outrageously exclusive, brand new restaurant. He and everyone else within a 500-mile radius wanted to eat there, hence, the four-month waiting list to get in.

Without hesitation, I said, "No problem. I can get us in." Calling my bluff (damn he's good) he replied, "There's no way." Challenge accepted.

I have an overwhelming feeling I may go to hell for the trick I pulled, but with a room full of executives, I called the restaurant on speaker. Pressure cooker. Naturally I was a little panicked, despite having had a 100% success rate with this trick of mine. So, with everyone crowded around the phone, I sweet-talked us into the 7 p.m. reservation. Mission accomplished!

---

21 Chutzpah: 1. Unmitigated effrontery or impudence; gall. 2. Audacity; nerve. (http://www.urbandictionary.com/define.php?term=chutzpah)

22 Pussyfoot: To go about timidly and cautiously (alludes to a cat walking carefully). (http://idioms.thefreedictionary.com/pussyfoot+around)

23 Baller: A thug that has "made it" to the big time. Originally referred to ball players who made it out of the streets to make millions in the pros, but now is used to describe any thug that is living large. (http://www.urbandictionary.com/define.php?term=baller)

As soon as the restaurant gave me a confirmation and we heard the dial tone, the room went nuts; everyone was flipping out—there were cheers and high fives everywhere. You would have thought we won the lottery!

The baller was in utter shock, but he knew right then, I could make the impossible happen!!! Did I mention, we won the business?

I wish I could share the secret trick with you, but then I'll never get a dinner reservation again! Not to mention, I am the vault.

SHOW 'EM YOU AREN'T AFRAID OF A CHALLENGE.

CONNECT QUICKLY

How quickly can you make a connection with someone? It better be fast; we rarely have the luxury of gaining someone's attention for more than a few minutes. Do something to be memorable: share a funny story, compliment them, tell a joke, embarrass yourself, whatever you need to do to stand out from the pack. People are being pulled in a million directions every day. How are you going to rise above the noise?

I was at a conference at the Ritz Carlton recently. I got on the elevator, and there were three men who had obviously just gotten back from California Pizza Kitchen. They were carrying their leftovers to their rooms. I broke the awkward, inevitable elevator silence (why, why, why is that particular silence so deafening?) by commenting on how delicious their food smelled. One of the men fired a compliment back and said how good my perfume smelled. I said, "Yes, perfume and onions, always a yummy combo!" and we all laughed.

It was a nice surprise to find out later one of the men on that 60-second elevator ride was the CEO of a Fortune 500 company with whom I was trying to get a meeting. Albeit brief, it was a memorable encounter and made landing the meeting a snap!

Easy as 1-2-3

1	2	3
Do Not Check Your Phone	Do Make Eye Contact	Speak Up! Break The Ice

SEIZE THE MOMENT TO CONNECT WITH PEOPLE BEFORE THE MOMENT'S GONE.

HARNESS YOUR MOMENTUM

It's one of those weird things, but once you land that first meeting, it's somehow easier to get the second and third and so on. Confidence is contagious (like laughter and enthusiasm!) and people tend to gravitate toward a hot commodity.

When I sold TV shows, I motivated myself like the star quarterback on game day. In my case, the Heisman Trophy would be to create a bidding war for my show and close a deal with the best TV network for the job. Once one of the big networks accepted a meeting, the others jumped on the bandwagon. No one wants to miss out on the next big show (FOMO![24]). This is true in any business or social setting.

When you're trying to get traction and build momentum, land the first meeting with someone you already know. Tell the buyer who else you're planning to talk to and leverage the first meeting in your favor. Stoke a little healthy competition among interested parties by casually mentioning you're meeting with a direct competitor, and watch them scramble. This is a strategy you can take to the bank.

The power of momentum is working in your favor when you're winning and selling in succession. Success follows success, so the best time to set up meetings is when you already have meetings. If your leads go cold, it means you need to check your playbook and get a new game plan.

---

24 FOMO: "fear of missing out." The fear that if you miss a party or event you will miss out on something great.
(http://www.urbandictionary.com/define.php?term=fomo)

MAKE YOUR PITCH SEXY

Remember when we talked about collaborating versus pitching? Being in sales means you need to be creative about product positioning, and that's when pitching comes into play. Your relationships will remain collaborative, but don't forget, no business: no Choos.

Every product has the potential to be sexy. It's just a matter of how you spin it to the buyer. Even the most seemingly ordinary of things can be exciting. For example, a computer chip may not sound all that thrilling (unless you're into that kind of thing). But, that little chip is what makes your computer 10,000 times faster, better, and more efficient. With that information, the chip becomes a very sexy product. If you're passionate enough about what you're selling, you can inspire the dull to be shiny!

Giving people what they want (and need) is sexy! Trust me, people get very turned on when the stars align, and a beautiful business relationship is consummated.

WHAT MAKES A PITCH SEXY?

 Being authentic.
Better to be an underdog than full of shit. Recognize your limitations.

 Offering a sneak peek. Everyone thinks they're special when they get a first look.

Saving money (efficiency).

 Intriguing listeners with visual presentations that appeal to the senses.

 Saving the world.

 Creating attractive packaging. Both the product and the people selling it should be in stylistic alignment.

> MAKE YOUR PRODUCT ATTRACTIVE
> WITH CREATIVE POSITIONING.

ONE SIZE DOES NOT FIT ALL

Successful business development executives must be flexible in their approach. You need to bend according to your audience and sometimes that means doing so on the fly. You don't want to be so rigid the client can't do business with you. Give the client an opportunity to customize a package that fits their needs.

When I sold TV projects, I crafted different pitches depending on the network. The people at NBC had an entirely different set of parameters and priorities than those at HBO.

STRATEGIES FOR FLEXIBILITY:

* ✴ If the client wants to lead the meeting, adjust your presentation to be more responsive;

* ★ Encourage questions for an interactive dialogue. Conversations lead to better outcomes;

* ☆ Be open and creative in the moment to foster a new approach regarding client needs;

* ✴ Go off-script for a customized presentation and make the client part of the process; and

* ★ If there are cultural differences, play it safe by following their lead on what is appropriate (I would not go to first base with the executives in a predominantly conservative country—respect the culture.)

Be flexible
to be sure you are meeting the client's needs
and not your own.

THE NO-PITCH PITCH

All hail the no-pitch pitch! Often the way to get client buy-in is to let them take the lead on collaboration. It's not uncommon for my clients to ask, "How can we work together? Who do we need in the meeting to make it a success?" See what happened there? I allowed my prospect to draw the conclusion. It was his/her idea.

Recently, a friend and I were comparing notes about conference pitching strategies. Usually, the only reason anyone would be at such a conference is to learn, sell, or both. I had just been at a conference, and I didn't make a single pitch to anyone. Everyone had some agenda, but mine was to be silent.

Because I felt no pressure to pitch or sell, I was completely at ease, and others picked up on that. It also created an air of mystery, which caused my "It Factor" to skyrocket. It was almost like the prospects were scratching their heads and wondering, "Why isn't she selling me anything? What does she have that I want? Is it that good? I want what she is *not* selling me."

Having no agenda works! After the conference, I received follow-ups from several members of the C-suite and continued the agenda-free banter before talking business. In a work environment, people always tend to think you want something from them, and maybe you do (and vice versa), but it doesn't have to be the first and only thing you discuss. The no-pitch pitch is an excellent strategy for getting to the boardroom. It's disarming, attractive, and obviously, totally irresistible.

DITCH THE PITCH.

PARTY CRASHER

Getting in occasionally means going where you're not invited. I'm not ashamed to admit, I've crashed a lot of parties in my day. This is easier than you may think. If you show up, look confident, and act like you're supposed to be there, you'll be handed a drink and hors' d'oeuvres just like everyone on the guest list. Half the time, people think I'm the one *hosting* the party I crashed!

It's always easier to crash the boardroom when you're not angling for an invitation. You can ask for whatever you want while sipping martinis at a party. If your confidence is faulty, have that first drink and get some liquid courage! (But remember, no one likes a sloppy drunk. Channel your inner Jackie O. Leave your inner Snooki at home.) The connections made in a social environment are the ones that stand the test of time. A few drinks, a festive setting, and the emotional crush is on!

My goal is to hang out with the most fascinating people, period. I don't always know who they are, but once I figure it out, I ask to join their table. Anyone can do this—it's about finding your own style. Personally, I take the confident approach and simply walk up to them like I own the place.

I behave the same way when it's time to sit down in the boardroom: first come, first served. If there's an open seat at the table, sit in it without hesitation! Remember musical chairs? You'd better grab that seat before someone else does, or you're out of the game.

Go back to the old playground days. You spot a kid you want to hang out with; she's got something you're drawn to—a cool joke or some impressive swing set skills. You just know she's got "it." Well, jump on the monkey bars and show 'em what you've got. Together you can make something happen.

If you wAnt A seat At the TABle, TAke it.

CORPORATE WALLFLOWERS

Corporate spending is no secret, and it's not uncommon for companies to throw down wads of cash to rub elbows with potential clients. The really mind-boggling thing is how many people are intimidated by approaching the client and striking up a conversation—even when they have a captive audience. Some companies pay the equivalent of my salary or more per event to get the attention of the high rollers—but then, they don't even talk to them. It's simply irresponsible (not to mention embarrassing) to spend hundreds of thousands of dollars to sponsor an event or host a cocktail party and then clam up.

An easy way to get your money's worth
IS TO FOLLOW A FEW SIMPLE STEPS:

★ Identify the potential client;
★ Approach the potential client;
★ Introduce yourself as the host; and
★ Thank them for coming to your event.

Seems obvious? I know. Even when my company is paying for a sponsorship, and it's our cocktail party, I've seen my associates talk only to each other. They are not behaving like hosts, even when we've paid to get access to the guest list. If you're sitting at a dinner table, stand up and introduce yourself to every person sitting there. Model professional behavior and others will follow suit. Don't travel in a pack with your associates! You can find one buddy from your company to tag team with, but that's it. You're not cool because you have 30 of your own people surrounding you. Trust me, you couldn't be more amateur. It screams "inefficiency" and it makes you completely unapproachable.

The most brilliant minds seem to go completely blank when it comes to networking. All the money and brains in the world won't get you the business if you're paralyzed by fear when the time comes to socialize. There is no reason to buy your way into an event if you don't know how to connect with the people in the room when you get there.

Be a good girl (or boy) and engage everyone! Most people are not social butterflies, so if you are, take responsibility for others. Lots of interesting people are shy until they are in a safe environment. You know what they say about the quiet, conservative types—they're the wildest behind closed doors!

DON'T SQUANDER EXPENSIVE OPPORTUNITIES TO CONNECT.
GET OUT THERE AND MINGLE.

HOW TO GO VIRAL WITHOUT GETTING AN STD (SALES THROUGH DONATIONS)

In business, you *want* people to talk about you behind your back. Let others do the PR for you. It's more cost-effective and powerful than renting a billboard promoting your own fan-tam-u-lous-ness.[25] Going viral doesn't need to be dirty.

Referrals are preferred over vetting new business all on your own. People would rather work with people they know or have some link to than with a stranger. When you're introduced to a prospect through a personal recommendation, that prospect's confidence is elevated. Your friends and clients are your greatest asset in filling your pipeline. Typically referrals have 50% conversation rate vs. a cold call rate of 2%! If you have a good relationship with a client, ask for a referral.

★ Hit up three of your favorite clients and ask them to be your "go to" references;

☆ Ask a few clients to write recommendations on your LinkedIn or other business networks; and

★ Gather testimonials and splash them on your website.

LET YOUR CLIENTS BOOST YOUR SALES ACUMEN BY DONATING TO YOUR FUTURE SUCCESS.

FANTAMULOUS

---

25 **Fantamulous:** A combination of "fantastic", "Tami", and "fabulous" which is my personal version of awesome. For a deep dive on this word (and others like it), see "Being Fantamulous" in Chapter 14!

CHAPTER 5

Keeping it REAL

CROTCH SHOT

There have been some pretty hilarious (and humiliating) moments peppered throughout my career in business development—too many to include in a single volume of stories and advice—but this is one of my favorites.

I was getting ready to pitch a TV show to the president of ABC. He's a real hotshot, but I knew him from way back, when we were pups. We grew up in the industry together, and a group of us used to meet for a regular happy hour.

Getting the meeting was a piece of cake; I just asked. I was with my two studly business partners, which made it three men and me. It's not unusual, unfortunately, to be the only girl in the room.

We were led into a massive office and sat down in a circle on unusually low couches. These couches were so low and so comfortable, that getting myself into a power position was a little awkward. I leaned forward and teed off the pitch. Just then, I glanced down and noticed my fly was completely down, exposing my bright electric blue panties. FUCK. I was frozen and mortified. I could not believe I had forgotten to zip up my pants after going to the bathroom in the lobby. To make matters worse, it was laundry day and I was wearing my comfy cotton GAP daily affirmation "Inspirational Underwear." What was today's message? "YOU ARE BEAUTIFUL." Are you fucking kidding me? You are beautiful?!?! What was I going to do? They could clearly read my underwear.

I couldn't even start the pitch because all I was thinking about was my "beautiful" crotch right out there for the room to see. Well, I thought, screw it. I stood up, my crotch now at eye level, and said, "I guess this might be the most original icebreaker you've ever seen," zipped up my pants, and sat back down. Everyone looked at me like I was fucking nuts (which I am) and had a good laugh. With that, the energy was great and the pitch went better than we had hoped. Although we sold the show to another network, that went down as one of the most memorable pitches in history.

It's always good to have an icebreaker
—planned or unplanned.
Turn an embarrassing moment
into an opportunity to put everyone at ease.

EVERYBODY POOPS!

It's human nature to be intimidated by success, but let's face it—everybody poops. We all put our pants on one leg at a time (and sometimes, we even forget to zip them). Having money and being successful doesn't mean you are any less vulnerable to insecurity or failure than anyone else. So, let's not see titles; let's see each other.

What's with all of the egos? I can't think of one person who can justify having an inflated ego. There's nothing wrong with confidence, but there is a huge difference between believing in yourself and being a jerkoff. If you think you're better than the valet, better than the waiter, better than your associate because you have a higher-ranked position or a bigger bank account— then you're just an asshole. Those 20-year-old dropouts could easily have the next "big idea" . . . and maybe even your job in a few years.

Come back to earth. We all know you're just acting like a big turd because you're scared. I don't know one person who's not insecure about something. Over the years, I've had many friends and associates confide in me about their job insecurity and the fact they felt under-qualified for a promotion. We're usually our own worst critics, and it's common to worry we're not smart enough, not good-looking enough, not worthy, etc. Everyone does this, from the top on down and back up again.

Once you realize we're all similar, regardless of titles and salary, it's so much easier to be, accept and love who you are. I've found it really helpful to create a list to blur the lines so you don't let insecurities drive your actions.

I'M NOT SHITTING YOU

Since we're all on the same page with the fact that everybody poops, here's one for you! I was the guest of a client at a fancy, full-sponsored, fabulous weekend event in Miami with art, fashion, food, and parties. When I arrived at the airport, I got a text message from my client that said, "What time are you getting here? We're going to Calvin Klein's private party!" In the car, I was already figuring out what to wear. I was not going to miss this!

Within 20 minutes, I found my clients in the hotel lobby and we were off and running. Once we arrived at the party, I was laser-focused on the Dom Perignon and watching the who's who of celebrity and fashion. Both of my clients kept encouraging me to eat something because they had gone to dinner before I arrived, and the Dom was going down like water! I ate tons of tiny little food, clearly intended to keep the models from tipping over. I put on my best inner-supermodel attitude because there was no margin for error in my skin-tight black strapless dress.

The night was completely fantamulous until about 3 a.m., when my stomach was gurgling enough to wake me up. Next thing you know, I couldn't get to the bathroom fast enough. Turns out, I got food poisoning from the tiny model food. Things went from bad to worse. I was dying because the hotel didn't have any anti-diarrhea medicine and I couldn't leave the room to get any. My clients (both male) kept calling and eventually I had to tell them what was going on. With my pride and confidence at an all-time low, I asked them to (PLEASE) pick up some Pepto-Bismol for me at the drugstore.

They hooked me up without too much grief and later that afternoon, I met them at the Soho Beach Club. I was terrified of how far the bathroom was from the beach cabana where I was trying my best to carry on and schmooze. It was a traumatizing day, but

I managed to stay fantamulous by drinking Pepto-Bismol from a martini glass.

I didn't want to miss any of the VIP activities (FOMO), so I pushed on into the night. Maybe it wasn't the wisest choice, but I decided to wear my super-tight white jeans. They looked really hot (if I do say so myself) and they were perfectly appropriate for Miami. The guys were laughing their asses off when they saw what I had on.

"It's been a shitty day in South Beach. Don't you think that outfit's a little risky, Tami?" They asked as they giggled like fourth graders on the playground. I knew the risks. I knew the probability of shitting my white pants was at an all-time high, but that's the price you pay for looking good. Thank God, that didn't happen, but everyone had a really good laugh at my expense. I was literally the "butt" of that inside joke.

SOMETIMES THE JOKE IS ON YOU.
YOU HAVE TO BE ABLE TO LAUGH
AT YOUR OWN EXPENSE.

DANCE Like ELAINE

Most people hold back because they don't want to look like an ass, but there is nothing better than seeing someone let it all go and dance like Elaine from *Seinfeld*.[26] Sometimes, letting other people see your geeky side is just what it takes for them to open up. When I have people over to my house, I turn on the music and start dancing. I don't worry about what I look like; I just let go and let it rip. When I put myself out there, other people start to feel comfortable. Inevitably someone else will want to let their hair down too. It makes me so happy because it means they:

- ✳ Felt safe;
- ★ Leapt without a net;
- ☆ Stopped worrying about how they looked;
- ✳ Got out of their own heads;
- ☆ Were not stressed or worried; and
- ★ Were free!

Amazing things happen when people are given permission to be themselves, even if it's just for a few seconds. No one needs perfection; it's stuffy and creates too much pressure (and it's boring)! We should all dance like Elaine!

I think dancing is one of the reasons Ellen DeGeneres is so successful. She gets everyone up and moving within the first ten minutes of every show. She sets the tone for people to celebrate their individuality and just have some fun.

It doesn't matter who you are or what your title is—people need to feel safe before they will participate. Whether you're in the living room or the boardroom; take a chance! Be geek chic!

BE THE FIRST TO LET GO AND HELP OTHERS FEEL SAFE.

26 https://www.youtube.com/watch?v=DY_DF2Af3LM

THE MOONWALK.
YES, AS IN MICHAEL JACKSON

Dancing is a great equalizer. Unless you're John Travolta or Juli-anne Hough, most of the rest of us are pretty pathetic. We may aspire to have the moves like Jagger, but the reality more closely resembles the chicken dance or the hokey pokey.

Sometimes the most memorable moments spring from inside jokes. I found one of my best friends and most influential mentors all because of Michael Jackson. Somehow, after four glasses of wine, we were both convinced we could do the moonwalk, and it got competitive fast (as the moonwalk often does). We had an impromptu moonwalking race all the way from the bar to the valet and laughed so hard we almost peed our pants. We looked ridiculous, but felt safe enough with each other to make monumental, King-of-Pop sized asses out of ourselves.

Not only are we lifelong BFFs because of it, the dance-off was profitable; that client ended up giving us a 108 million dollar deal and an open line to call him for any advice, which is worth (way) more than my commission!

BE SILLY, HAVE FUN,
BUST A MOVE!

HOT MESS With ORANGe FEEt

Does it seem like I go to a lot of conferences? Yeah, I agree. Being out on the road as much as I am is an endless stream of opportunities to keep it real! I was scheduled to attend a conference on a cruise ship in the Bahamas (which doesn't suck) immediately after a grueling business trip to New York City. We were going to an exotic private island, and a bikini was inevitable. Looking paler than Casper, I decided I should bust out a spray tan before I went anywhere.

I explained to my spray-tanning technician that I had a four-day lag in New York and wanted my "deep olive tan" to last until the Bahamas trip. She nodded and promised to layer it on thick. Perrrrrfect. After leaving the salon, I felt more like a tangerine than an olive but was confident the tint would settle out over the next few days.

I got to the first conference in NYC in true Tami fashion: a hot mess, slightly disheveled, spilling coffee, juggling my bag and bagel, squeezing into the middle row. I happened to be seated next to the VP of a major consumer products company who was also the keynote speaker. We exchanged intros and pleasantries in typical conference nicety-speak.

When we had a break, I wasn't in the mood to start mingling with strangers and started looking around for a familiar face. The VP was the only one I saw, so I headed over to him. This guy looked directly at me and said in his thick Italian accent, "Do you realize that you have orange feet?" I looked at him, and then at my feet, then back at him, and felt that I owed him an explanation. I tried to explain how pasty I had been and hoped he would identify with my plight and condone my trip to the tanning salon. I assured him that I requested a deep olive tan and the woman just went too far. I'm sure this kind of thing happens to men in Italy all the time.

He pondered for a moment and said, "For the record, you might think having a tan is attractive to others, but you just look like an Oompa Loompa." I could do nothing but laugh. Was this a test to see how cool I was? Would I be offended and storm off? Or was I able to laugh at myself? This was the start of a beautiful friendship, and I thought the whole situation was a riot. I looked like Anne Hathaway in *Bride Wars*.

DON'T TAKE YOURSELF TOO SERIOUSLY.

HOW TO HANDLE FUCK UPS WITH COPS

Commuting is an inescapable reality when you live in L.A. I drove from my office in Hollywood to my house in Santa Monica every day for almost seven years. And every day, I avoided one stoplight where there was always a major cluster fuck at the main intersection. I always turned left onto a small side street, so I could cut through a residential neighborhood and get around the traffic. One day, a sign appeared that said, "No left turn between 4-7 pm." Ugh. Apparently, the neighbors didn't like my shortcut.

Out of habit, I continued to turn left into that neighborhood and quickly fell straight into a police trap with several other cars. Well, shit, I was in the wrong, I just forgot. When the cop pulled me over, I rolled down my window and said, "I'm sorry. I forgot that sign was posted." The cop asked for my driver's license and crazy Tami-Nado[27] took over. I said, "Listen, I'll flip you for it." In disbelief, the cop said, "What?" I said, "Let's flip a coin and if I win, I don't get the ticket, and if you win, I get the ticket." He lit up, "Okay!" So we flipped, and I lost . . . shit, fuck! "Okay," I said, "two out of three." He looked at me in utter shock, but definitely entertained at my chutzpah, and agreed. Sigh. I lost again . . . shit, fuck, fuck!

The cop asked what I did for a living, and I told him I worked in the entertainment industry. We went back and forth for a minute, shooting the shit on a random Hollywood side street, both almost forgetting why we were there. Then, to my surprise, he said, "Alright, I'll let you off with a warning. Don't do it again."

Sharknado

---

27 **Sharknado** is a 2013 made-for-television disaster film about a waterspout that lifts sharks out of the ocean and deposits them in Los Angeles.
(https://en.wikipedia.org/wiki/Sharknado)

"Ah!" I said, "Thank you, thank you, thank you! I thought I was a goner! Especially since I lost the bet *and* I look like a hot mess without any makeup!" His reply was, "Please! With a personality like that, who needs makeup?"

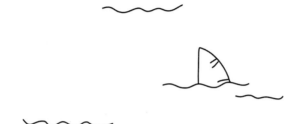

Own your mistakes.

RUNNING INTO YOUR EX(ES)

Breakups happen every day, even in business. But it's not every day that you're sitting in the same room, at the same table with two ex-clients, is it? Yup, that happened to me at a marketing conference. Shit got real! Out of a table of six, myself included, I had worked for four, two of the four contracts expired, one was looking to hire us, and the other one was my lone existing client. Yikes.

Some think the key to success is keeping your current clients, your former clients, and your potential clients as far away from each other as possible, but that is totally unrealistic. So, how does one deal with this crazy awkwardness?

When confronted, don't cower or sink into your chair wishing you could blend in with the upholstery. Do the opposite. I run up and give them a hug and kiss with an all-forgiving attitude. I immediately go back to first base, just as I did at the first meeting. Even if they aren't working with you anymore, they don't want to be in that awkward situation either. So save everyone the pain and jump in!

BE THE BIGGER PERSON
AND TAKE CHARGE OF AWKWARD ENCOUNTERS.

TO BE, OR NOT TO BE?

"Be the change you want to see."
-GANDHI

Whether you are Gandhi, the CEO, an associate, or just starting out, behave in the manner in which you want to be treated. Make people better by knowing you; because you believe in them, they will be capable of doing more. It makes sense: what comes around goes around.

To be	Not to be
Someone to hang with	Someone to be avoided
Likeable	Mean
The good guy	Unapproachable
Consistent	Unreliable
Honest	Deceptive
Respectful	A douchebag
Curious	Fake
On time	Late

Not everything is roses and butterflies and when shit happens, how you approach the stakeholders speaks to how you do business. Whether it's a disagreement, a mistake, or a negative result, you must maintain open communication. We all have to deal with people every day, and we need support from our associates and our clients. The goal is to keep your relationships intact for future opportunities. Don't avoid unpleasant topics. None of us are mind readers.

AVOIDANCE DOES NOT MAKE AN ISSUE DISAPPEAR;
IT ONLY DRIVES OTHERS TO MAKE ASSUMPTIONS
BASED ON THE INACCURATE OR INCOMPLETE INFORMATION.

WHAT ARE PEOPLE SAYING
BEHIND YOUR BACK?

"It's not what you gather, but what you scatter that tells what kind of life you have lived."

\- GOLDA MEIR

When you behave in a way you hope others will emulate, you have slightly more control over what people's perceptions are of you. What impression do others have of you? When you leave the room at a meeting or a business event, what do you want them to say? I want them to say positive things about me, as I'm sure we all do.

At a sermon over the High Holidays[28], my Rabbi talked about how we don't die with money in our pockets; we die only with our reputation. It was an eye-opening reminder for me and I think of it often when I meet new people.

What is the legacy you'll leave in this life? I'm not being morbid; rather, I'm promoting an exercise in self-examination. Are you a good person? A funny person? Someone people trust? Are people going to share beautiful memories of you or are they going to say you were a mean-spirited, selfish asshole? The choice is yours! Believe it or not, you control the conversation behind your back. Give people a reason to sing your praises.

---

28 **The High Holidays**, or **High Holy Days**, in Judaism, strictly, are the holidays of Rosh Hashanah ("Jewish New Year") and Yom Kippur ("Day of Atonement"). (https://en.wikipedia.org/wiki/High_Holy_Days)

CHAPTER 6

The FLUFFER

THE **ULTIMATE** FLUFFER

Urban Dictionary's definition for "fluffer": (noun) Pornographic film industry employee who is responsible for keeping male performers aroused (usually via oral sex) between takes during a shoot.

The use of this term has recently entered the business vernacular. For example, a real estate "fluffer" is a person who stages homes for viewings to make them more attractive to potential buyers.

I'm not trying to brag or anything, but I've been called "The Ultimate Business Development Fluffer" by a few of my friends. The reason being is that I usually engage in some pretty heavy foreplay before we even get into the boardroom. By the time the meeting starts, the emotional erections are fully engaged—including mine! The first sit-down meeting is comparable to the first sleepover in a new relationship. You've established that it's a good fit and you're taking things to the next level.

There is a reason when you go to a live TV show like Jimmy Kimmel's, there's an opening set with a different comedian (the fluffer) before the show starts. As the audience becomes engaged, they begin to smile, relax and laugh. The fluffers have successfully laid down the framework and amped the audience up for the main event. In essence, I do the same thing—I get people warmed up for a successful meeting by making them feel good and pumping up their confidence.

THE IMPORTANCE OF FOREPLAY
CANNOT BE OVERSTATED.

BRAG

I love to make other people look good—not just to their face—but in front of an audience. The more people hear me brag about them, the better they feel about themselves (and the better I feel about making them feel good). The added benefit is that doing for others reflects positively on you.

I have a friend who is brilliant at bragging openly. He's a very successful entrepreneur, but he's also super humble. He makes himself look good by surrounding himself with all of his "favorite people." He's incredibly genuine and when he says, "you are the best in the business, and you are my favorite person," you are! I don't care if he introduces everyone the same way because he's sincere. Whenever I see this guy, I know that by association, I am going to have a good night.

I had a conference call recently with a total schmoozer who happens to be the executive producer of a big talk show. He introduced me to his associates by saying "she's the girl who makes shit happen." I loved hearing that, even though I barely know the guy. He said, "I knew the minute I met Tami she would get what we're doing, and you can consider her family." I thought, "Holy fuck, did this guy take a page out of my book?" When I like someone, I always treat them like family! Luckily for him, his instincts were correct.

If you want to test the theory, bring one of your fabulous friends with you to a networking event and brag about each other to whomever you meet. You both will be having so much fun; you'll get an instant kick-start because people will be magnetically drawn to you. You'll start your own little movement and you won't have to toot your own horn.

Another approach is to create your personal fan club, aka Team

Tami. Who's the president of your fan club when you're at a meeting or out and about? Who is going to brag openly about you and root for your success? We all need people to hear us the same way we hear them, and we need them to go to bat for us!!!

ATTRACT POSITIVE ATTENTION
BY ROOTING FOR OTHERS' SUCCESS.

SMILE ☺

"A smile is a curve that sets everything straight."
—PHYLLIS DILLER

If someone is smiling at you, how do you not smile back? Seriously, try it. It's impossible! Smiling is an invitation to a conversation; it's infectious, and it makes people warm up to you instantly.

My girlfriends and I had a theory that we would meet more boys if we practiced the smile therapy technique. We made up our own little market research project to test it. We'd walk into a room and smile at everyone with zero discrimination, I mean ZERO. Wow, it worked like a charm. Total bozos[29] (and one or two babes) approached us within a matter of minutes to comment on our great smiles. We were having fun, we were approachable, we were happy! No bitchy resting faces allowed. (Body language, people!) If there is anything that can counter negativity, I say, SMILE and go for it!!

---

29 **Bozo:** An incompetent person, especially in new companies. Bozos have a net negative effect on morale and profits, and everyone knows it. (http://www. urbandictionary.com/define.php?term=bozo)

I smile so much people comment on my teeth, which is funny, because I had to have a few front teeth removed, due to really bad TMJ.[30] It's as good as new, million-dollar smile (just ask my dentist, who's enjoying his new beach house) and I get a ton of use out of it!

Have you ever noticed people who don't smile look exactly like *Droopy*? (MGM knew what they were doing in the '40s!) It's like gravity has a special hold on them. If you're having a bad day, as everyone does, attempt to turn the frown upside down, because no one wants to hang out with a Debbie Downer. People choose to work with positive and friendly people. What better way to let them know you're one of them?

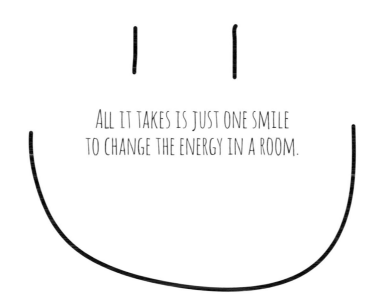

ALL IT TAKES IS JUST ONE SMILE
TO CHANGE THE ENERGY IN A ROOM.

---

30 **Temporomandibular joint disorder (TMJ):** A disorder of the temporomandibular joint(s) that causes pain, usually in front of the ear(s), sometimes in the form of a headache. Grinding or clenching the teeth due to stress is a frequent culprit. (http://www.medicinenet.com/script/main/art.asp?articlekey=5731)

2 SECONDS 2 FEEL GOOD

It takes two seconds to impact someone's day in a positive way. Tell the people around you something funny or inspirational, or send a flattering message to someone you're thinking of. You don't have to be a philosopher or a motivational speaker, just send a quick pick-me-up. The key is to be sincere!

How hard is it to help someone else feel good? It's the easiest thing in the world! I do this all day long: I compliment my gardener on my beautiful plants, I tell my intern how proud I am of her, my niece how well-behaved she was on our sleepover, my girlfriend how smoking hot she looks in her new heels, my Mom how much I love her, and on and on. When I believe someone deserves a compliment or a lift, I tell them. Make a habit of it!

2 SECONDS 2 FEEL GOOD EXAMPLES:

* You made my day!
* Why didn't I think of that?
* You're my favorite person on the planet!
* I couldn't do my job without you!
* Your haircut looks amazing!
* Hello, gorgeous!
* You are beyond talented!

I'll show you how well compliments work on me. This is my favorite text from a client:

"Hey Girl, It's been a while. Wondering if you are still stunning the masses with your combination of brains and beauty? Let's talk business!"

I perked right up at the **"BRAINS and Beauty"** part. Hello, Hello! I said it out loud a few times just to hear how great it sounded—music to my ears. Now that, my friend, is how you send a 2 seconds 2 feel good message!

My client sent me that text because he was trying to charm me and, I'll admit, IT WORKED!!! A bunch of us were headed to the South by Southwest Festival, and if you didn't have access to the right party and the right people, you might as well just get dropped off at Disneyland and be told, "Start networking!" His text jump-started the emotional currency model (see Chapter 8 for more information on this subject), and I gave him complete access to all my parties and relationships. Of course, that was his intention, and it only took two seconds for a win-win, feel good.

A LITTLE FLATTERY WILL GET YOU EVERYWHERE.

TAMI FEVER

When people feel good about themselves, the strangest thing happens. They transfer their good feelings to me and start to think I'm brilliant. Honestly, it's like I fed them three pills of ecstasy. (Fluffing and ecstasy, now we really are shooting a porno!) They're hallucinating! When I give them compliments, I start to appear better than I am. Maybe I am mentally infectious? Most people would feel high as a kite after hanging around someone that makes them feel like a billion dollars. (FYI, billion is the new million, just like 40 is the new 30!)

I remember a business partner's husband used to say, "There she goes again. They have Tami Fever. We need to prescribe Tami-Flu!"

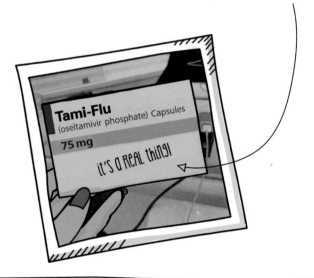

Tami-Flu
(oseltamivir phosphate) Capsules

75 mg

it's a real thing!

EMOTIONAL ECSTASY IS TOTALLY LEGAL IN ALL 50 STATES.

THE BIRTHDAY CONFERENCE

I'm not one of those people who is way into her birthday but, just my luck, I had to attend yet another conference on my birthday one year. We've all been there. The day feels kind of special, but then at the same time, it doesn't. It sucks to be tied up with work, and away from the people you know and love when the day rolls around. C'est la vie!

When I got to the conference, I was immediately invited to the VIP client's table. I was introduced to the moderator/host of the event, and we became fast friends—bonding over her gorgeous St. John skirt and a mutual friend within her organization. Somehow it came up that my birthday was the following day (I may have mentioned it 😊), what a drag, etc. She said, "That sucks, but hey, I may call you out in the morning when I am doing my intro, so make sure you show up!" I laughed it off, assuming she was kidding.

To my surprise, the next morning, still half-asleep, I hear, "So hey, I met this very cool girl last night from Blankety Blank. Her name is Tami Holzman and today's her birthday, so make sure you wish her a happy birthday." This became an ongoing gag for her onstage, like a comedian, every time she needed a transition, she would say, "Have you wished Tami a happy birthday yet?" It was pretty fantastic. You can't pay for that kind of publicity! It may as well have been called "Tami's Birthday Conference."

To top it off, my company was sponsoring a luncheon at the conference and my favorite associate, who had missed the multiple birthday shout outs, was speaking. Without knowing about my previous bout of free press, he announced my birthday to the crowd, complete with a photo of me at a party, blowing a kiss and wearing a hot pink fedora and boa!

I thought spending another birthday traveling would be a buzz kill, but it ended up being a blast. There were more than 600 potential clients, all celebrating my birthday (they probably just wanted a reason to party, but they were all in!).

After my birthday conference, I set up a dinner with the fabulous woman to thank her for making me look like a star. A beautiful dinner was a small price to pay for being the belle of the ball, and we've remained close friends ever since.

FREE PUBLICITY. PRICELESS.

DADDY'S GIRL

I have to give credit where credit is due: I learned a hell of a lot about sales from my Dad. He could pretty much charm the pants off anyone. I envied that about him. We used to get the best rooms in all the hotels where we stayed because he knew how to work the system and we always got upgraded. Being with him was like being with the Godfather, minus the crimes (plus, we're Jewish, not Italian). I was mesmerized watching my Father in the heat of the action as he gave a $5 oscillating plastic fan to the hotel manager as a thank you. That guy acted like my Father had just given him a diamond Rolex! Pops had some mad skill sets to pull that one off.

Lucky for me, I got that gene and, like my Dad, I also get upgraded at hotels and get the best seats in restaurants. It all comes down to how you treat people. I only give them what they want most: a hug, validation, and my billion-dollar smile!

☆

MAKE EVERYONE FEEL LIKE A BILLION BUCKS
AND SHOW THEM YOUR APPRECIATION
FOR HOW THEY MAKE YOU FEEL.

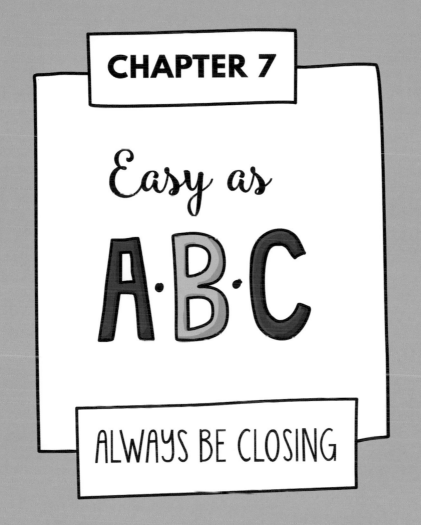

CHAPTER 7

Easy as

A·B·C

ALWAYS BE CLOSING

WHEN YOU'RE NOT IN THE MOOD

If charming gets the business, it's pretty much a 24/7 job. I'm a work ambassador and, on some level, I never turn work off. If I am in a crappy mood (which happens), I am ineffective.

If you're in a legitimately bad place, it's okay to share your feelings with your inner business circle (within reason). Use discretion with what you share, but let others in a little. People will surprise you. I've been a rock for my colleagues, and they've definetly returned the favor.

Some of the most successful people I know are also the most vulnerable. I won't speculate as to why, but I appreciate that they choose to let me in. It's endearing, human, and real because it's difficult to connect with people who put on a façade all the time.

Of course, there are times when the temptation to wallow in self-pity becomes a threat to your earning potential and your natural fantamulousness. In which case, nip it. You gotta walk away from the Ben & Jerry's — get out of those old pajamas and show'em what you're made of. There are times I would rather stick needles in my eyes because I am not in the mood to network. Then I remember one word: commission. Money is a strong incentive to take a shower and deal.

Here are a few things to try when you absolutely have to rally:

⭐ Put on your most expensive outfit. If you don't put it to use, you've wasted thousands of dollars;

⭐ Find another schmoozer to hang out with;

⭐ Ask one of your co-workers or assistants for follow-up deadlines and start dialing;

⭐ Identify something you really want to buy and use it as an incentive. Don't let yourself buy it (e.g.: new car, new furniture) until you land the next big deal;

⭐ Get your hair and makeup done;

⭐ Call your most inspirational friend and let him or her boost you;

⭐ If you're at an event, hit the bar first and loosen up over a cocktail. There's always someone there who will get you in the mood; and

⭐ Read the entire collection of Tami-isms at the end of this book.

PUT ON YOUR BIG GIRL PANTIES
AND SUCK IT UP.

MORE IS MORE

I don't know where people came up with that whole "less is more" bullshit. More is more and, in my experience, more is better. Luck is a probability game and the more real connections you have, the more meetings you have, the more you get paid and the more you can demand, and the more shit you can buy and the more fun you are going to have!

I rarely talk about business when I'm at business networking events. My preferred ratio is 95% social to 5% business. If you have enough deals cooking and enough contacts, you will get the business. But, obviously, you cannot sacrifice quality for quantity. Just as more is more, shit is shit, so aim high.

I was talking to an account executive recently and asked her if she liked sales. She immediately said, "No, I don't like business development. I like to pitch, but I don't like converting." Wow. I understand the hustle of business development is not for everyone and people like the high that can come from pitching a great idea. But for me, the converting is so interesting because you're closing deals, which is locking in your commission.

Yes, there is a ton of pressure throughout the cycle (opportunity, pitch, close), but once you have a healthy pipeline, the pressure is off conversions. At that point, you need to switch your focus to growing your contact network. Remember, it's a probability game! No one likes to sell or be sold to from a desperate place. Once your pipeline is filled, it becomes so much more fun to have people call you to solve a problem for them. The best way to get business is when it seems like you're doing them a favor when they need your services, not the other way around. Of course, it should be mutually beneficial. The key is to keep building your contacts, because people, more is more.

A POSITIVE PIPELINE IS A BUSINESS DEVELOPMENT EXECUTIVE'S BEST FRIEND.

ACQUAINTANCES Schmaintences

When assessing your popularity scale, how many people do you think would consider you an acquaintance or a close business contact? An acquaintance is someone you have seen ten times at a conference, but don't know anything about them, aside from the name on his or her badge. Whenever someone remembers my name and something personal about me, such as where I live or what I like to do on the weekends, I am always a bit flattered. It means I was memorable to that person, and I stuck out from the crowd.

During a business event, I was introduced to a CEO and said, "Oh, it's so nice to meet you, Joe Blow." In return, he gently reminded me we had met before, which launched me into a "shoot me now" tailspin. I wanted to bury my head in the sand, but instead, I downed my glass of chardonnay and instantly apologized for not remembering him. We got over the awkward start and started chatting; he's a very cool dude (he owns a vineyard!), and it turns out, he lives down the street from me.

After a few minutes of shooting the shit, I said, "We may have met before, Joe Blow, but we've never had a conversation. I would have remembered you are my neighbor! I am so glad we have this connection, and we should get together when we're back in L.A."

I faced my embarrassment head on and walked away with my pride and his respect. He is not an acquaintance schmaintence anymore!

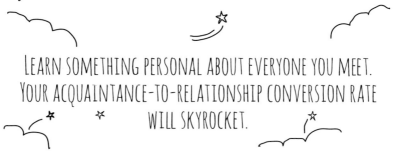

LEARN SOMETHING PERSONAL ABOUT EVERYONE YOU MEET.
YOUR ACQUAINTANCE-TO-RELATIONSHIP CONVERSION RATE
WILL SKYROCKET.

TAKING ONE FOR THE TEAM

My coworkers always joke about how I will readily take one for the team, and it's true. With an "always be closing" mindset, there's not much I wouldn't do to move the ball forward for our team and land a sale. Now before you jump to conclusions, that's *not* what I'm talking about! I'll share a couple of stories with you so you catch my drift.

We were at a client dinner with about ten people, and I was the sole female. The main executive was a little smitten by me, and not only did he order my meal for me, he actually cut my food and fed it to me! I can tell you; the whole table shared my pain as they watched their boss embarrass the hell out of himself. There I was, just trying to endure the evening with as much class as possible: laugh, accept fork from the executive, chew food, smile, and refrain from stabbing executive. Ay yi yi, that guy! What was he thinking?

Another time, at an industry event, with a different group of people, I was having dinner with a bunch of new contacts and one of my associates. During the first course, an acquaintance of a friend's husband came over to say hello. The hello turned into an unwanted flirtation and quickly escalated to inappropriate. As he was finally leaving, he leaned over to give me a kiss on my neck (who does that?), but he actually gave me a hickey in front of everyone. For a girl who typically doesn't get embarrassed, I was traumatized. Seriously? A drive-by hickey! I try to be friendly to everyone, but come on! Friendly doesn't warrant a hickey with my salad.

Now if that's not taking it for the team, I don't know what is. Try explaining that one at the table. Luckily I didn't have to; my look of pure horror said it all.

Sometimes just being a girl
lends itself to taking one for the team.

I NEED SOMETHING

Many years ago, the VP of a Fortune 100 company brought me in to consult on some partnerships he was considering. A few years later, as luck would have it, I ended up meeting the chairman of that company through my old business partner. He was lovely! He said to me, "I love what you're doing. If you ever need any help with anything, please don't hesitate to call me."

The next morning, at 9 a.m., on the button, I called him. When he picked up the phone, the first thing out of my mouth was, "I don't know what I need yet, but I'm sure I need something." He ended up being the lead investor in the company I worked at for seven years, and we've been amazing friends ever since.

ALWAYS ACCEPT OFFERS OF HELP, EVEN IF YOU DON'T NEED IT YET.

TAKE THE BUSINESS

My focus is always on closing, so I don't waste a lot of time thinking about my competition. Of course, I'm aware of competitors, and, in some cases, I'm even friends with them, but I don't obsess about their stealing my business. When I was in the entertainment industry, I never once thought, "Oh no, Steven Spielberg might show up with an idea and then we'll be competing." I know I can get to the right people, so I tend to think about issues that might impact them. Do I have something they want to buy? Is the idea creative enough for their company? Is it marketable for their audience? The bottom line is: if I have something great and it's different, the customer will buy it.

Even though I don't sweat it, unfortunately, the corporate world—and sales departments in particular—are anchored in a competitive marketplace. The reality is you either win the business, or you lose the business. What I've learned is that winners *take the business*. How do they do that? By acting like they *already have the business*. This goes hand-in-hand with walking into the boardroom and acting like it's a done deal. (Business Duh'velopment, people!!)

Corporate America spends a ton of time and money worrying about and studying the competition. And yet, the whole corporate system is set up to fuel competition through the RFP (request for proposal) process. Does this dynamic somehow validate the opportunity as "more real"? The whole thing seems ass-backward to me.

I've heard senior executives tell our clients, "Hey, let us know when you have an RFP. We'd love to participate." What? They just asked to be benchmarked against another company. Why on earth would they do that? A better approach would be to bypass the RFP process altogether and take the executive out to lunch to find out what they need. This seems painfully obvious to me.

When a C-level executive sets up a meeting with his or her team on our behalf, it's already teed up. In that case, I tell the team we appreciate the opportunity to work together, and I make sure they know we've already gotten the green light to move forward. This way, you close the deal in your opening sentence.

OTHER SAMPLE CLOSING TECHNIQUES

Safe close
"Let's pick a pilot project to get started and test our relationship."

Start the paperwork close
"We'll send the paperwork over, so we can move forward seamlessly."

Be responsible close: Show them why working with you will make them more responsible, (i.e. faster, better, cheaper) and explain how it will be irresponsible not to work with you.

Schedule another meeting to close: "Let's set up the next meeting to hammer out the details and costs."

Assume the close: "I can't wait to work together. We're going to kick ass!!"

Show them how much fun it is to close: "It's about time we started working together. I am beyond excited to partner with you!"

No lose close: "Try it. You'll like it, but if you don't, I'll give you an out!"

Innovation close: If what you are selling will save them money, let them know how they can use the savings!

 Tee-it up close: "Have our lawyer talk to your lawyer for the close."

 Ask what they want to close: Give it to them.

 Cute as a button close: Make puppy dog eyes and ask for the deal.

 Fluffer close: Flatter them and pump their ego until they cave in and sign.

 **Courting close:** Take them to dinner and romance the hell out of them.

 Dramatic urgency close: "Buy now and save the company (or the world)."

Drunk close: Go to a bar, consume four drinks (minimum) and close.

Regardless of how you close, the business is there for the taking. Get creative and above all, get a signature!

☆ ☆ ☆ ☆ ☆ ☆ ☆

Approach each client as if you're the only game in town. If you've made the clients' needs your top priority, the competition doesn't stand a chance, anyway.

☆ ☆ ☆ ☆ ☆ ☆ ☆

THE MAVERICK PROCESS

Someone once asked me to write down my "process," and I thought, "Are you kidding me? Have you not seen me in action? What is my process? How do I put my process of building relationships into a report?"

We should be less worried about the "process" and more focused on the *results*! No? How many new relationships did I introduce to the company? How many were converted into deals? Did we hit our sales goals?

It's difficult to work for people who have become accustomed to environments with clear and defined assessments of what "success" means. These people utilize objective variables to form an equation in order to analyze gains. When you are in a subjective space, there is no equation to win business, but I gave it a shot anyway.

FOCUS ON THE RESULTS, NOT THE PROCESS
(BUT DON'T TELL YOUR BOSS I SAID SO).

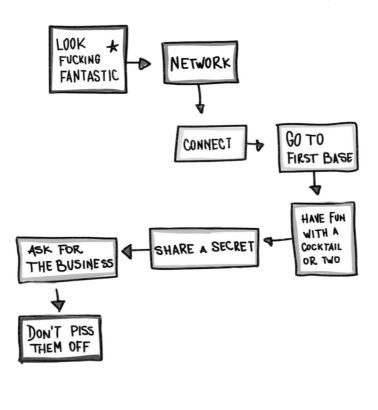

CHAPTER 8

EMOTIONAL CURRENCY

THE EMOTIONAL CURRENCY MODEL

When I make other people feel good, it gives them confidence; confidence yields inspiration and inspiration yields rewards. This cycle is not exclusive to me; it's reciprocal. When others compliment me, my confidence increases; my confidence then leads me to become inspired, and I reward those who inspire me. The best part about this cycle is the rewards last a lifetime. It's not about sucking up; it's about encouraging others and calling attention to their hard work. It is an emotional bank account with unlimited spending.

Sample Business Rewards:

☆ Boardroom meeting;

☀ Referrals;

★ A new job;

☀ A new friendship;

☆ A new mentor;

★ Looking good in front of your boss;

☀ Free work advice;

☆ A meal, a martini, a trip, etc.;

★ A raise; and

☀ A party invitation.

Here's an example of how the Emotional Currency Model works: I was at a massive marketing conference, and an adorable, former American Idol contestant was performing Motown. He was so good; it was literally impossible to sit still in my front row seat. Surprisingly, the rest of the audience was not as enthusiastic. As he played on, I was the only one chair dancing and encouraging him. How awful for this guy! It takes immense courage to get on stage and perform in front of a group of people.

The crowd's lack of response made my heart hurt for him. After two songs, he acknowledged me shyly, even though I was howling, singing, and clapping. "Ah fuck it," I thought. I got right up and started dancing alone. Then, thank god, this random girl joined me! It was awesome! We were rocking out and having the best time.

When the performance was over, so many people approached me and said they wished they had the courage to get up and dance. My so-called "courage" was more about supporting someone than it was about confidence in my dancing ability. It spoke to my character, apparently, because that night I had more leads for business opportunities than ever before. All it took was a happy dance in front of 500 strangers. Totally worth it!

HAVE AN UNLIMITED SPENDING ACCOUNT BY MAKING PEOPLE FEEL GOOD.

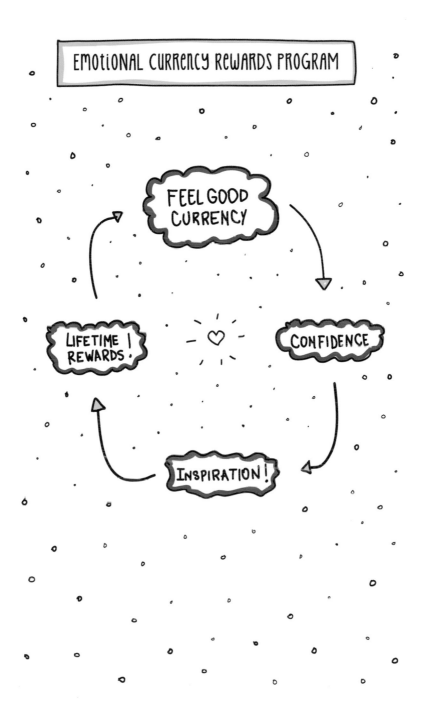

THE PUTZ[31] NEGATIVE CURRENCY MODEL

What does the model look like in reverse? The Putz Negative Currency Model leads to low morale, which yields poor work performance and feeling like a big loser. Worse, you have to live with the fact you are a Putz.

People don't want to work with or be around a Putz. Misery loves company, so the people associated with the Putz are most likely unhappy and, thus, Putzes by association.

When people put you down and make you feel bad about yourself, they are employing manipulative tactics to control you and damage your self-esteem, which gives off negative energy. We typically resent the people who cause us pain, and we don't want to go out of our way to do nice things for them.

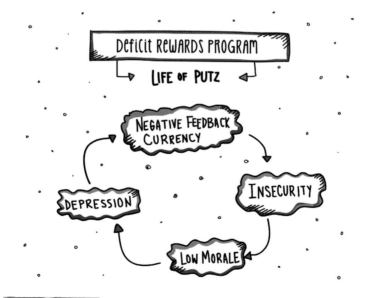

---

31 Putz: stupid, ignorant person; someone who doesn't pay attention to anything going on; one who makes stupid remarks
(http://www.urbandictionary.com/define.php?term=putz).

WARNING

Behaving like / associating with
a Negative Putz may cause an increase of:

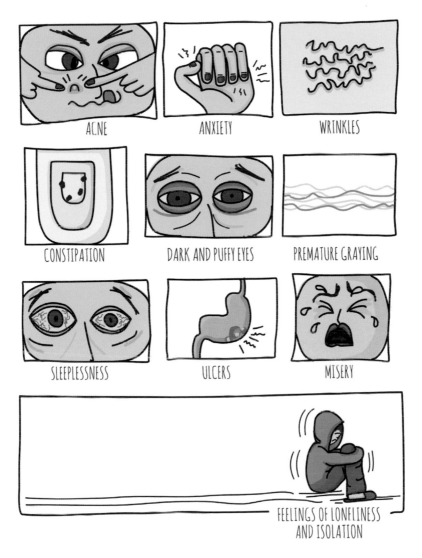

YOU CAN BE A NEGATIVE ASSHOLE, BUT THEN YOU HAVE TO LIVE
WITH YOURSELF, AND YOU'LL HAVE NO FRIENDS.

THE VAULT

Trust is the cornerstone of any good relationship, and the more you know about someone, the deeper the relationship becomes. For this reason, and as soon as possible, I take my clients out for a social meal. I strategically choose restaurants that scream, "Have a glass of wine!" (Or three.) This is the beginning of the "share your secrets" recipe: set up the ideal environment where you can relax and have fun.

We all have something to share, so why not create a circle of trust with a client? The reward is twofold: you'll establish rapport and inspire a symbiotic relationship based on honesty, confidence, and trust. When you let each other in emotionally, it leads to transparency in business too. The backstory of someone's life is key. If you can get someone's personal history . . . Game changer! You're in. The relationship is solidified, not to mention you get to see how interesting and insane people's lives are. Trust me, if you start doing this, you won't need TMZ.

Naturally, I gravitate toward people who are a bit flawed. Perfect people are boring, which is probably why we all love TV characters like Don Draper from *Mad Men*, Carrie Mathison from *Homeland*, and Louis C.K. all brilliant and complicated—my favorite combination!

When people confide in you, they trust you. A couple of my friends have nicknamed me "The Vault" because people know they can come to me with anything in confidence, and it doesn't go anywhere. I am a top-of-the-line, steel storage unit full of stories from the most brilliant, slightly fucked up group of clients (BFFs) and friends. Let's face it: gossiping is just not a good look. The reason I have so many friends is because I keep my mouth shut. While I'm loud, and you can hear my raspy Demi Moore meets Fran Drescher

voice from three blocks away, I am not a gossip. There's a difference. Gossiping sends the message, "I will talk about you, too,
when you aren't around. I can't be trusted." Get your thrills because
you are charismatic, not because you benefit from knowing other
people's secrets.

CREATE A CIRCLE OF TRUST.

BE A CATALYST

Making connections to build your network is step one to increasing your business value. However, connections aren't just about you and your business—utilize your relationships to be a catalyst for others to work together. It takes nothing away from you to introduce two people or give a referral for business outside your sector. My connections are layered and multi-faceted. If everyone's interests are served, I win in the long run and so do they.

It's in my DNA is to help others and I do that by building and intertwining my collective networks. My mind works like a giant forensic map. You know the kind investigators use in crime dramas? My map is filled with potential business associates (not murder suspects) who have commonalities. By connecting others, my web is strengthened.

Make this a common practice, and when it becomes a habit, you'll be recognized as a power player who can point anyone in the right direction. Moreover, your efforts to help others won't be forgotten—especially if the connection yields positive results. What you get in return are emotional currency lifetime rewards, which, as you know, don't expire.

My matchmaking Yenta[32] skills kick into overdrive when introductions are made on pure future potential. I've said to colleagues, "You should meet so-and-so, she's doing something right up your alley. There might be collaboration at some point." Don't be shortsighted and see only the immediate needs.

Identifying your forensic map of business contacts is easier than you think! I get paid to be able to sort through the puzzle in my

---

32 **Yenta:** The name of the matchmaker in the Broadway musical hit of the same name.

head, but having access to social currency gives everyone a little cheat sheet for who you have in common.

LinkedIn is a public Rolodex on steroids, and I use it all the time. Top things I love about it:

- ♥ It's a great way to follow-up with new contacts. Plus you get to see all of their contacts, too;
- ♡ You can join interest groups to become more visible to your target audience—selling ice to an Eskimo? There's a group for that;
- ♥ You can make yourself irresistible. Write your profile like a marketer;
- ♡ You get to ask your most fabulous and powerful friends to write you a recommendation;
- ♥ You can find out where people live, work, what they studied, and more;
- ♡ You can use keywords to find other people with similar interests;
- ♥ You can be an influencer by writing and sharing articles on your public feed or with your private groups; and
- ♡ You can be your own "Six Degrees of Kevin Bacon" by using the "how you are connected" tools.

CONNECT PEOPLE WITH THE RIGHT CONTACTS, SO THEY CAN SUCCEED TOO.

GOING THE EXTRA MILE (IN FIVE STORIES)

1

The airlines only allow two carry-ons, so your purse is crucial. I have this fantastic, gorgeous black handbag with gold hardware. It not only carries all of my personal shit (which is a lot), it also holds my laptop, my tablet, and a notebook. This handbag is timeless and elegant and (if you take your computer out) you can use the bag from day to night.

I was in Europe on business and a girl who quickly became my BFF said, "I have been looking at your handbag for days, and it's truly beautiful." So I decided I would let her in on my big secret. I had been eyeing the large Muse YSL handbag, but I couldn't get myself to spend $1,700. Then, I stumbled across my new amazing bag at J. Crew. It didn't have a big flashy label on it, and it was perfect. I got 20% off, so the bag cost me less than $300 (I love a ba'gain). The Sales girl told me that J. Crew uses the same factory in Italy as Hermes!! Shut the fuck up! Now I carry this bag with pride as if it was Hermes!

This girl lives in Geneva, and when I saw J. Crew was offering 20% off again, I called and offered to get the bag and ship it over. But she beat me to the punch. On a recent trip to the States, she got one for herself. Needless to say, she was happy I would have gone out of my way to get her the bag. Not only had I made a new friend, but I also landed a meeting my company had been trying to get for years with the top dog executive at the largest pharmaceutical company in the world. That top dog executive was my friend from Geneva.

2

I was pitching a sports reality show called "Super Agent" with my partners (those two smart, studly guys that every girl wanted to date and every guy wanted to befriend or date). We nailed the pitch every time, which naturally resulted in a bidding war. We chose the winning network based on their follow-up alone. The NBC team sent all three of us a basket of cookies. Each cookie was in the shape of a different sports ball (a football, a baseball, a basketball, etc.) and decorated accordingly with a note attached that said, "The ball's in your court." That is a perfect example of how to win a tiebreaker. They went the extra mile to communicate just how badly they wanted to make the show. Their effort was so personalized, thoughtful and creative, we knew they were the winning choice.

3

One of my clients has a son who recently moved to L.A. When she told me, I insisted she give him my phone number so I could be his emergency contact. She had tears in her eyes as she said, "Do you know how much that means to me as his mother?"
I didn't offer my number so I could call in a favor later; it was pure impulse! She is a fantastic lady, and I truly would do anything for her. I'm a nurturer at heart and want to take care of others. Since I have no kids, I compensate by being a mommy to the world.

Consideration for others goes a long way in life—not just in business. It doesn't take much to make a difference in someone's day.

4

Case in point: I was flying to Europe, and as I approached the gate, the plane crew was waiting in the gate area. A passenger walked up to them carrying an assortment of bagels, coffee, and drinks. They were ecstatic over the gesture and immediately upgraded him to first class (to one of those stinkin' private rooms in the front of the plane!) for the 20-hour flight! NOW THAT IS HIGH EQ! Kindness is contagious. I'm just jealous I didn't think of it first. There's always next time. Go big or fly coach!

5 ——————————————————————————

When I was growing up, my Grandpa Leonard would send my Brothers and me articles he came across that he thought would interest us. He cut them out of the newspaper, put them in an envelope, and scribbled a cartoon caricature after the "Love" salutation that looked like him. Every time I got an article in the mail from him, it made me feel special. Because of him, I'm a person who goes the extra mile; it's part of my DNA. Now when I read something in the paper or online, I email it to my family, friends, and clients. It's a way for me to say, "I am thinking of you."

SHOW PEOPLE
HOW MUCH YOU APPRECIATE THEM
BY GOING THE EXTRA MILE.

STEP BACK THE ATTACK

Those of us who are fortunate enough to have a high EQ know difficult conversations need to be handled delicately. A girlfriend of mine was telling me about some troubles she was having with her boyfriend. He felt like he was regularly being attacked and unappreciated. She was complaining about some of his annoying habits. As I listened to her, it sounded like they both had valid points. But what she wasn't doing was reassuring him. I told her it's important to make people feel safe before offering any sort of criticism. I suggested she start with, "First, know that I love you," *then* tell him what was on her mind. This way he wouldn't immediately take a defensive position.

The same goes for business. I've had clients approach me when they're unhappy with our work. This information is always best received when they open on a positive note, i.e. "First of all, we enjoy our working relationship. We want to figure out where the mistakes are occurring and why. We want to be able to pinpoint the issue, maybe it's communication or planning, so we can resolve it quickly." Now, isn't that easier to swallow than, "We need to talk. I am not happy. This is not working. Your team is not delivering."

When people feel attacked, the natural human instinct is to defend themselves and attack back. Everybody just calm down and think about your delivery.

♡

♡

WHEN APPROACHING A NEGATIVE SITUATION, ALWAYS BEGIN WITH REASSURANCE.

♡

♡

♡

SWEETBITCH

I am not America's sweetheart, but I am a total fucking sweetbitch. I usually put other peoples' feelings before mine, which has occasionally come back to bite me in the ass. Some pretty sneaky people have burned me. Unfortunately, the majority of people are looking out for their own interests: Are they getting the sale? Are they getting the credit? Are they getting full ownership? I get it; you have to put yourself first, blah blah, but there's got to be a balance.

While I do believe you get more with sugar, you should never sacrifice your own needs. So, is it better to be a sweetheart or a bitch? I think I need to learn to be a little bit of both, a sweetbitch. You don't have to roll over and aim to please everyone 100% of the time, but there's a way to balance honey and vinegar.

PRINCESS WARRIOR GODDESSES, UNITE!

"There is a special place in hell for women
who don't help other women."
—MADELINE ALBRIGHT

Otherwise known as The Queen Connectors or The Bad Ass Girls of Business, we chicks need to encourage each other and stick together! If you don't see the value in what the other X Chromosomes bring to the table and can't figure out how we can support each another, then you should be ashamed!

Stay away from the Stilleto Stompers: the women who are threatened by you and who will go out of their way to sabotage your success because of their insecurities. (Also known as "Mean Girls." Thank you, Tina Fey!)

Women currently hold 5.2% of Fortune 500 CEO positions and 5.4% of Fortune 1000 CEO positions.[33] By those numbers, it still appears that men run business— minus the fact that women control 80% of consumer spending and 45% of American millionaires are women. It's estimated that by 2030, women will control as much of two-thirds of the nation's wealth; this could be you! So, who runs the world? Girls! (Thank you, Beyonce!)

Women control trillions of dollars in spending, and that fact alone should make you feel powerful. I'm sure you've splurged on a pair of shoes in your life. Well, good for you! Look who's controlling business?

---

33 http://www.catalyst.org/knowledge/women-ceos-fortune-1000

While women still make less than men (GRRR), there are areas where we are thriving, particularly within women-owned and operated companies. A recent *Forbes* article, "11 Reasons 2014 Will Be A Breakout Year For Women Entrepreneurs," cited the impressive growth: 57% in $10-million-plus-women-owned firms.[34]

In addition to the nearly 50% growth rate among women-led businesses, there's been a spike in financial backing for the ladies. Angels and venture capitalists are only two of the stakeholders who have increased their investments in women-led businesses (by 12-20% since 2012). Hey, if we can't get paid what you are worth, then fuck it, girls, you can just start your own company and pay the men less. (Ha, nah, men should get what they are worth too! Equality!)

Personally, I am proud to be an angel investor and an advisor in Laurel and Wolf, the online interior design technology company with an amazing female founder; she even started a networking group called the Bad Ass Girls of L.A.! Supporting other women is the number one way to be a Princess Warrior Goddess.

With women holding the purse strings, there are endless opportunities to increase the number of female entrepreneurs. Women are also jumping in on the investment side, as they should be, considering 60% of high net worth women have earned their own fortunes. Women also control more than half the investment wealth in the U.S. according to *Women and Money: Matters of Trust* by Mary Quist Newins.

While we own 50% of the wealth, we make up less than 10% of early-stage investing. Think about it—if we increased that number to just 15-20% of women's capital (currently sitting all lonely in

---

34 http://www.forbes.com/sites/geristengel/2014/01/08/11-reasons-2014-will-be-a-break-out-year-for-women-entrepreneurs/

some bank) and redirected it to investing in early stage, women-led companies, the landscape would be transformed. It is a pivotal time for young, hungry, female entrepreneurs to thrive and shift the paradigm.

Jack Zenger and Joseph Folkman, of *The Extraordinary Leader*, say women "tend to combine intuitive and logical thinking more seamlessly; they're more aware of the implications of their own actions." They also said women breed employee loyalty and respect by nurturing the staff. Isn't that true? When you love your boss, and you feel respected and supported, don't you do better? Go the extra mile? Women, according to studies, not only know this; they practice it, which leads to employee retention and rapid growth.

"Fifty percent of female Millennials (ages 18-35, born in the 1980s—early 2000s) see themselves as entrepreneurs. And, the girls of Generation Z (those born after 1995) are the most connected, educated, and sophisticated generation in history. They don't just represent the future, they are creating it," according to social researcher Mark McCrindle, of Sydney-based McCrindle Research.

Since we control consumer spending, we are THE influence when it comes to spending categories—and it's not just makeup, shoes, and clothing (although I do love all three). Why are men so shocked when women are interested in other industries, like autos, technology, and sports?

When we were pitching our sports show, the men in the room were stumped when it came to attracting female viewers. I looked around the room, and I was the only woman there. Women not only make up 40%+ of the female fan base in mainstream sports (i.e. NFL, NBA, MLB, NHL), they are also the consumers and the gatekeepers of the household. If a guy wants to go to a game, whose permission does he need? His wife! You often hear your guy friends say, "She's the boss." Now, let's bring that same spirit to the business world.

Women have the ability, the money, the opportunity, and the skill set to run the world. Period. What do we need to do to make that happen? Drawing from my personal experience as a woman in the workplace—at times, the ONLY woman in the workplace—as a female entrepreneur, and as an independent woman who takes no shit from anyone (well, unless I'm taking one for the team), but knows how to get more with sugar, I know that **my fellow Princess Warrior Goddesses need to:**

1 - Support other women;

2 - Stick together;

3 - Push ourselves to do better;

4 - Celebrate one another;

5 - Educate the younger generation about female power;

6 - Stop young girls from bullying and cutting each other down;

7 - Encourage fearless confidence. We can. We will. But it won't happen if we're too afraid to take calculated risks and question the status quo;

8 - We need to be confident in our abilities. The drive and work ethic is there, but what good is it if we're too scared to jump;

9 - Attend girl power events; and

10 - Find female mentors.

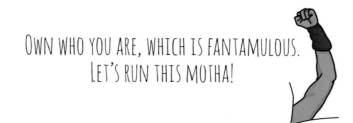

OWN WHO YOU ARE, WHICH IS FANTAMULOUS.
LET'S RUN THIS MOTHA!

GROW A VAGINA

What do you have to lose by walking up to someone and introducing yourself? A bruised ego? Ah, poor thing. I say, suck it up! Usually, if you approach someone in a chill manner without being a pest, they will (at the very least) be polite in return. Worst case, you're told to fuck off. Best case, you get a meeting or even better, a new BFF.

I have huge balls for a girl, but I wish I was even ballsier. I'll tell you, the ballsier you are, the easier it gets. There is no guarantee people will like you immediately, but I highly doubt you'll get slapped in the face. As much as people hate rejection, they don't enjoy rejecting others either. The fact is, you never know what kind of reaction you'll get. It's a gamble, and the outcome is not always fun. What's your incentive to potentially make an ass of yourself?

Let's get back to balls. You can use them in many ways: you can be a ball-boy or a ball-buster, or you can just have enough balls to march up to total strangers. Unfortunately, life is still a bit of a boy's club, and businessmen can sometimes resemble fraternity boys. They like to show off and test you, but if you can hang with them, you're in. I say put your balls on the table. The women are usually the ballsiest in the group, anyway.

Betty White says, "Why do people always say, 'Grow some balls'? Balls are weak and sensitive. If you really want to get tough, grow a vagina! Those things take a pounding!" God, I love her! If men think with their penis, imagine how much knowledge you have in that powerful vajajay!

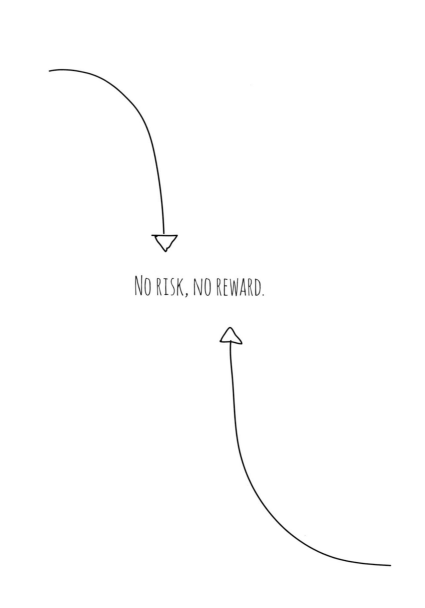

No risk, no reward.

GENDER (IN)EQUALITY IN THE WORKPLACE

According to Sarah Silverman in her "Gender Pay Gap Solution," every year, the average woman loses $11K to the wage gap. Over the course of her career, that's almost a "$500,000 Vagina Tax," which is why she said she decided to get a sex change.

The case for gender equality in the workplace continues to be a battle. We want equal opportunity, equal pay, and equal respect! It's astounding that this is still an issue. Hundreds of studies have been conducted to determine what and why the gap is merely shrinking instead of disappearing altogether. The question remains, when will we catch up?

> *"Gender stereotypes in the workplace are common; whether brazen or subtle, they exist nonetheless. They are detrimental to professional women and it needs to end in order for us to break through the glass ceiling. However, when viewing these characteristics holistically as 'traits' instead of 'stereotypes,' it's clear that, regardless of gender, there's a spot on the team for everyone. Executives are just now realizing the balance of these traits is the recipe for success."*
> —DREW GANNON, *THE FISCAL TIMES*, MAY 25, 2012

If a woman exhibits behavior perceived as "tough," she's a bitch. If a man is tough, he's a strong leader. If she cries, she's emotional. If he cries, he's a wimp. Blah, blah, blah, you've heard it all before. Is there a place for stereotypes? Is it a matter of opinion? Perhaps the bitch can de-escalate a bad situation better than anyone. Maybe the wimp is the perfect salesman, complete with a sensitive and disarming demeanor. What if these stereotypes weren't such a bad thing? Before you open your laptop and rip me a new ass on social media, hear me out.

The Fiscal Times article breaks down gender differences in the workplace based on results provided by various researchers. In general, research shows "typical female traits" like being a team player, and the ability to exhibit empathy, are useful and necessary in the workplace. Additionally, the "typical male traits" such as a focused, logical approach to problem-solving, and directness are equally important. Does this mean we can only find them in women and men, respectively, because that's what society and tradition tell us? Further, if you do happen to fall into the stereotypical traits that match your gender, is that a problem? We need to change people's perceptions of these traits, not try to change ourselves.

Several studies perpetuate the claim that women, independent of age, are more emotionally intelligent than men. While many of these exclude other variables, such as socioeconomic status and other demographics, the consensus has been that women exhibit stronger scores in areas of managing, perceiving, facilitating, and understanding emotion. However, one study conducted in Spain showed while women scored higher, the gap decreased with age. As men get older, they become more emotionally intelligent.[35] While they haven't caught up to women, the gap has decreased. Will they ever catch us? Maybe by the time we make as much money as they do.

> *"To every woman who gave birth to every taxpayer of this nation, it's our time to have wage equality once and for all in the United States of America."*
> —PATRICIA ARQUETTE, 2015
> Academy Awards acceptance speech

---

35 http://www.researchgate.net/publication/257236324_Gender_differences_in_emotional_intelligence_The_mediating_effect_of_age

LADIES, USE YOUR INHERENT SUPERIOR EMOTIONAL
INTELLIGENCE TO DEMAND EQUAL PAY.

GUY'S GIRL

Studies suggest women, in general, have more emotional intelligence than men, but, if you win the men over on an emotional level, you're 75% of the way to winning their business. Men don't often get the chance to feel safe and open enough to share their feelings. This is a huge opportunity for us to gain their trust. Why not start there? Men rarely show their vulnerabilities to other men, so girls; you need to jump all over this advantage!!!

As one of my favorite male associates pointed out, lots of men have a mommy complex and don't like to say no to girls. There is nothing wrong with taking advantage of men's psychological childhood issues or your female powers to get a meeting. Men want to be Superman, Batman, Spiderman, Prince Charming, Robin Hood and, at times they want to take you on their magic Aladdin carpet ride! Let them open up to you as a confidant. Be empathetic. Play into your strengths of understanding emotion.

Are you a guy's girl? Take the Buzzfeed quiz and find out.
➡ http://bzfd.it/254xPBt

MEN NEED SHOULDERS
TO CRY ON, TOO, YOU KNOW.
BE THERE WITH BEER.

SEX It UP

I'll say it. I don't mind using my sex appeal and even a little flirta-tion to my advantage when it comes to getting a meeting with men. But, there is a fine line, the location of which you need to acknowl-edge to remain professional and not to intimidate others—espe-cially women. I love to watch other women use their femininity as part of a business strategy. I support it 100%. There is always something I can learn from these other girls!! The trick is to make sure you are treating everyone equally. But hell, if you're the only girl in the boardroom, take the advantage. Why not? Men do it all the time. Why can't women?

Remember, we can read the room better than the men. If you decide you need to brush up on the top five sports stories of the day, or turn on the charm, do it!

ALL IS FAIR IN LOVE AND WAR
—AND BUSINESS.

BAIT FISHING

I was entertaining some business associates at my house over Tami-tini's. One of my male BFFs asked, "So, did Joe Blow hit on you?" I said no because he really didn't. My friend said, "Impossible. He hits on everyone." To which I responded, "I don't think I gave him any leeway to do so." (Refer to the next chapter for advice on this.) "But, you know what he does do? He always uses me as bait at parties and flaunts me around in front of all the important CEOs and other decision-makers. He's not hitting on me, but he is definetly using me as bait!" My BFF said, "Tami, *we all use you as bait*." We cracked up all over our drinks.

Sometimes when I'm at a business cocktail party, the male to female ration is 100:1 ➔ 100 guys : 1 Tami. You've likely experienced a similar situation. In this scenario, don't be deluded into thinking you're the belle of the ball; the reality is, you are an earthworm on a hook. They are trying to score a conversation with another male executive. Guess what girls? Use it to your advantage. Be the best bait there is and charm the pants off of every male executive in the room. Line up those meetings, collect those business cards, reel 'em in ladies; you can laugh your ass off all the way to the bank. They're using you, so now use them.

YOU'RE ONLY BEING USED
IF YOU DON'T GET ANYTHING IN RETURN.

~ The Original ~
TAMITINIS
♡

YOU'LL NEED:

TOP-SHELF VODKA	St. GERMAIN	FRESH-SQUEEZED GRAPEFRUIT JUICE	FRESH MINT
ONE SHOT	HALF A SHOT	TWO SHOTS	HALF A CUP

THEN:

→ SHAKE until really chilled,

+ add candied grapefruit slice for garnish.

☆ Prepare garnish in advance —as they are a bitch to make.

→ (http://www.marthastewart.com/874109/candied-grapefruit-peel)

It's worth the extra effort because you will look like a rock star, Martha Stewart, Cocktail Goddess and people won't forget the special attention to detail. ツ

WHEN YOU GET Hit On

I used to feel insulted when I got hit on in business because I felt like the men didn't take me seriously. Well, once I hit 40, I thought, "Hell, yes! I've still got it!" The reality is, you spend more than 90,000 hours of your lifetime at work.[36] School and work are the most common places to meet your spouse.

The first thing I look for when I meet any man is, are they wearing a ring? Feminine instinct kicks in. I'm actually relieved when they are, because in my pea-brain head, I think they are "safe" (as if). I asked my friends who have recently been married if their new status has changed their business development role with male clients. They said they get more attention. Do men turn on the charm when there's less risk of temptation?

At work, we're all trying to put our best foot forward—building business relationships and wooing the clients. Everybody's usually feeling pretty good and confident. Confidence is attractive and attractions spring up between co-workers every day.

So, how do you deal with unwanted advances or a flirtation that has gone too far? And how do you get yourself to a safety zone without tarnishing a great opportunity? I'll let you in on my little secret: commission is my birth control.

---

36 http://www.businessinsider.com/disturbing-facts-about-your-job-2011-2?op=1

When someone is flirting with you:

 Take yourself out of the game. Ask if they are single and offer to set them up with one of your friends. This usually shuts them up.

 Sometimes people feel a false sense of closeness in the moment. Keep the conversation focused on business and gracefully wrap up the conversation.

 Laugh it off, as if they are not being serious and change the subject.

 Tell them straight up, "I'm flattered, but I'm not comfortable mixing business with pleasure. We can be friends." Offering to be friends will make any man lose his hard-on in seconds.

 Tell them you are in a relationship.

 Tell them you are celibate.

 Tell them you have a raging VD.

When someone comes on to you, don't freak out! It's flattering, even if unwanted. The most important thing is to keep the business relationship intact by being upfront. And above all, be respectful— we all have feelings.

WHEN YOU GET HIT ON AT WORK,
NIP IT IN THE BUD SWIFTLY
AND GRACEFULLY.

NO, I DID NOT GET MY PERIOD!

Hindsight is 20/20, but there will undoubtedly be times when you wish you had worn something else when you headed out that night. Maybe you're under or over-dressed, perhaps you're drawing unwanted attention, and I'm sure we've all had our fair share of wardrobe malfunctions. And sometimes, terrible, irreversible, gasp-inducing accidents occur. This was one of those times.

I was at the bar after an event in Boca Raton, which is where all of the action happens and the cool people congregate. I was gallivanting and holding court, acting like my usual self, talking to everyone, making intros, being the quintessential hostess with the mostess (even though it wasn't my party), etc. In walked this guy. He was dressed casually and looked pretty hip. He had a relaxed and laid-back air about him, like he was the funny guy everyone loves like a brother at the office. He made his way through the crowd and joined our group. After introductions and pleasantries had been exchanged, he bought me a glass of red wine. As he handed it to me, in slooooooooowwwwwwww moooooootiooooooon, it dropped to the ground and splattered ALL OVER my beautiful, favorite, perfect WHITE LINEN PANTS.

My attitude is usually, "Hey, it's not a party until somebody spills," but in this case, I was so bummed; not angry, just crushed. This was the first pair of white linen pants I had ever owned that made my ass look perfect! The poor guy was devastated and offered to replace them. I thought, "Even if I do let him pay for them (I would never), there's no way he can afford to." Those perfect pants cost me a small fortune. Boy, was I wrong. It turned out this unassuming guy was the keynote speaker at the conference! He was the global CEO of a major company.

Well, after he offered to pay for my pants, I said, "Don't worry. This little spill is going to wind up costing you much more than a pair of pants!" I won his business and that, my friends, was well worth looking like I got my period in the middle of a cocktail party! RIP: WHITE LINEN PANTS. I will always miss you.

Later, once I got to know him, he told his version of the story. He said he walked into the bar, looked around and said to himself, "Who can I hang out with in this place?" He saw me across the room and said, "Her. She's going to be fun." Guess I looked like an "It Girl!"

BE COOL,
EVEN WHEN YOUR FAVORITE OUTFIT GETS DESTROYED.

THINK LIKE BETTY WHITE

"Don't try to be young. Just open your mind."
—BETTY WHITE

Betty White is my hero, and not just because she told the world to grow a vagina. Is there a little bit of Betty White in Tami Holzman? I sure as shit hope so: she still works, she gets away with being dirty, she's gorgeous, and she owns it!

I had just been thinking about Betty White, when I saw an interview with her in *Harper's Bazaar*. At first, she speculated as to why she would be included in the "Fabulous at Every Age" issue, which is ludicrous. Then she went on to say she is not fabulous, but old; she's been blessed with good health and energy. She said she knew she was never going to look like Lana Turner, so why even compete in that category. She attributes her success to the fact that she doesn't complain, and she tries to accentuate the positive rather than the negative. She says, if you're complaining, you're no fun to be around and FUN is the name of the game!!

May we crown the Queen Betty White, the original Princess Warrior Goddess!

YOU'RE NEVER
TOO OLD
TO WORK IT.

CHAPTER 10

NEUROti-CUte
UNDERSTANDING YOUR SHit

RANT ON AGING IN BUSINESS

As I get older, ay, yi yi, I see everything so magnified. In truth, I am aging gracefully physically, but mentally—not so much. My mind knows the reality and I am fucking freaked out! How much longer can I really get away with this cute shit? If I am 40+, what is my maximum shelf life: 5-7 years? Is it possible to age like a fine wine or am I going to curdle like a carton of milk?

If I were married, would I feel insecure about aging? Who knows? My single girl journey has been and still is fun, but I wonder if I put the same effort into finding a man as I did into finding business opportunities, would I be married? And if I were married, would I be worrying about my cuteness expiring? Probably.

But if I were married, I would have a partner and we'd be in this whole aging thing together. Isn't that the point of marriage? To grow old together? But come on! It's not like marriage comes with any guarantees.

Then, it hits me, "fuck, shit, fuck . . . Am I going to be the most popular lonely old person?" Yes, I have great friends and yes, most of my friendships are for life, in business and on the personal side. I'm sure I will be undeniably popular, in my old age home, wheeling around in a metallic gold and glittered wheelchair with tennis balls in the spokes. I will have plenty of people to play Rummikub and drink fancy drinks with, but how long will I be working and successful? I don't know! This is some scary shit.

For a number of years, I was a big risk-taker. I was an entrepreneur and at times, I was a baller. At other times, I was broke—crazy broke (ask my parents)—but, of course, I was still flying private (on someone else's jet). When I decided to make a career being a connector and an influencer, I killed it! I was able to pay off all my debts, make a really good living as a high-powered executive, buy a beach house, wear couture and fully enjoy all the fruits of my labor. But the real question is: did I make enough money to pay the bills for the rest of my life? I doubt it!

It's getting dark in here. OMG, who the hell knew there was a dark side to being a cute, successful business development girl? WOW! Now I'm scared shitless just thinking about it! What does my future hold? At one point, there was a thought to make a Tami Jr. with my frozen eggs (yes, I said it, I froze my eggs), and I passed up a brilliant IVY League sperm donor, too. At least my little Tami would have rocked her IQ.

Why didn't I put more focus on aging or loneliness before? What am I going to do?? What is my exit strategy? What are my options? These are important things to worry about. Now I am worrying like it's a religion. I'm Jewish, so it actually is my religion. I am worried about worrying. Oh fuck, I need a Xanax. This is too much.

Wait, what if this book is my exit strategy? Nope, can't count on it, but I think it has some legs. Maybe everyone who reads it will want to hear me speak (or rant)? The only thing I can really rely on is my mad skill set in connecting people. I have to fully concentrate on it over the next few years, because there will be a shelf life for this aging, tall, cheeky, good-looking-enough broad (even if she's in denial).

What I don't want is to live in the shadow of my former (current) self. I don't want to hear, "Oh, you should have seen her when she knew how to work it. That girl was the best. She was legendary!" I don't want to be the girl that "was." I am a girl who knows better than to be a "has been" and, right about now, I think I should have focused on a backup plan!

I know I'm more experienced and savvy than the new, younger business development "It Girls" out there. My record speaks for itself, but doing what I do takes an insane amount of confidence— confidence that came with age, oddly enough. The confidence is rooted in how I present myself—in both appearance and attitude. Will it go away? Nah. I've never liked dairy much, but wine and I have a deep connection.

By the way, it's so annoying that men have a longer shelf life than women. Why do they become more rugged and sexy with age? (I secretly wish that their penises shrank and their wrinkles deepened, unless I am dating them, of course.)

FACE YOUR FEARS,
NO MATTER HOW TERRIFYING THEY MAY BE.

AM I A FAKE?

"I have written eleven books, but each time I think, 'uh oh, they're going to find out now. I've run a game on everybody, and they're going to find me out.'
—MAYA ANGELOU, NOBEL LAUREATE

Sometimes, I worry that people will find out that my life is a *façade*. My therapist and I talk about this a lot. Believe it or not, she says that all successful people feel this way. No one believes they are qualified to do their jobs. This has been true for me in the past. Regardless of what my previous jobs have been, I can clearly remember thinking I was not qualified for any of them.

I created a TV show, but I was not a writer. I represented talent but had no business judging what made talent good or bad. I owned a sports company and knew nothing about sports. I sold digital marketing production services but knew nothing about coding. Looking back over my career, I did know some general stuff, but more importantly, *I believed* in a lot of shit—shit that made me money!

If I believed in an idea or a person, nothing could stop me from getting in a room to sell it! Many years ago, a friend bet me that I could sell a dirty napkin for $5 in 30 minutes, and I sold it in two minutes! I've been an entrepreneur (feast or famine) for most of my career, but the common thread is being a connector, and I sell with enthusiasm and passion. So, how is that a *façade*? It's a fact!

Occasionally I still get paranoid, even though reason and sound judgment tell me otherwise. It hits me at random times when I'm out living my life, attending parties or events, networking, and selling to fellow big wigs with acronym titles, and I wonder if they will find me out. I think, "It's only a matter of time before they figure out that I'm just not that smart. They are going to realize that half the time, I have no fucking idea what I am talking about."

But, for some reason, I feel at home in this world. I figured out early in life that we all put our pants on the same way (and sometimes we forget to zip them up, and everybody poops). Everyone else has the same insecurities I have. They're worried the rest of us will figure out they don't know shit either! Who has all of the right answers, anyway?

Turns out I am not alone; 70% of all high-achievers suffer from the fear of being a fraud (even the ones from Harvard ☺)! This malady actually has a name: Imposter Syndrome.[37] So, great news, my life is NOT a *façade*. I just have Imposter Syndrome, which will cost me hundreds of thousands of dollars more in therapy.

DON'T SECOND-GUESS YOUR STRENGTHS.

---

37 **Impostor syndrome** (also spelled **imposter syndrome**, also known as **impostor phenomenon** or **fraud syndrome**) is a term coined in the 1970s by psychologists and researchers to informally describe people who are unable to internalize their accomplishments. Despite external evidence of their competence, those exhibiting the syndrome remain convinced that they are frauds and do not deserve the success they have achieved. Proof of success is dismissed as luck, timing, or as a result of deceiving others into thinking they are more intelligent and competent than they believe themselves to be. Notably, impostor syndrome is particularly common among high-achieving women,[1] although some studies indicate that both genders may be affected in equal numbers.[2]
(https://en.wikipedia.org/wiki/Impostor_syndrome)

WE ARE ALL VULNERABLE

When I date, I tend to date brilliant men—fucking brilliant men, the high IQ men. (Go ahead, ex-boyfriends, let the ego inflation begin.) These guys represent everything I think I am not. They got the straight As, the MBAs, the Ivy League degrees (many from Harvard). They're super-focused, fiscally responsible, etc. I immediately felt inadequate and "less than" in their presence.

I'm impressed with intelligence and clearly attracted to it, but I'm equally intimidated by it. I refuse to play trivial pursuit; the pressure sends me back to the SATs! Ask me to play charades—I can play charades! Then I realize there are all kinds of minds. My ability to hustle, get in the door, and tee-up the business requires intelligence—not more or less than, just different.

I used to tell my Mom, "Mom, I am totally insecure. I don't think I am smart enough for this person." She would tell me I was ridiculous, I was the only person she's ever known who can somehow connect with anyone, at any age, and make even the most awkward people feel fantastic and inspired. I hope to inspire anyone who has ever felt inadequate. Everyone has a unique skill set and, more importantly, we are all vital to making this world turn.

That feeling of inadequacy I felt around my ex-boyfriends is not unique to me. I know that now. EVERYONE feels vulnerable and pretty much no one likes it.

The reason most people don't ask for the big meetings is because they're afraid of being rejected. Vulnerability stirs our innermost insecurities, basically leaving us emotionally naked.

No matter how many influential books we read or motivational speeches we hear, we will inevitably feel vulnerable at times. It's human nature. Even if I act like the most confident person, so happy, so enthusiastic, please know that just isn't the reality all the time. I question myself on some level every day, and I'm not sure that's a bad thing! I ask questions like, "Did I handle that email properly? Did that point get across? Do they understand my value? Do they believe in me?" My therapist says this is totally normal, and I believe her. That's why I pay her the big bucks!

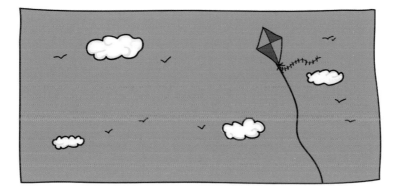

FEELING VULNERABLE IS INHERENTLY HUMAN.

IT'S LONELY AT THE TOP...
BUT THE VIEW IS MUCH BETTER

(This is my public service announcement for C-level executives everywhere. You're welcome!)

Have you ever noticed after a hotshot executive speaks at a conference, he or she is bombarded by people who rush the stage and try to pitch them? Then, the next day, you see that same hotshot walking or sitting alone? This has got to be such a crash and burn. Think about it; they're up on the stage, under the lights, they've got prime billing, everyone wants a piece of them, and then, bam, it's over. When the lights fade, and the speech has been delivered, and the books have been signed, and the cards have been swapped, the hotshot returns to his regular post, just out of reach of everyone else. And everyone else reverts to being in awe, and they're too intimidated to approach. The lonely hotshot takes his or her lunch alone by the pool.

Have a little empathy! It's intolerably negligent to let the hotshot sit around by himself, feeling unapproachable and insignificant. This is the very best time to approach, and it's all in how you position it. What do you have to lose? The worst-case scenario is you get the brushoff, or they're waiting for someone. But no matter what, they will feel needed, so there's really no downside.

This very scenario presented itself to me at a conference in Laguna Niguel. The day after the main event, I spotted the hotshot reading the paper and having lunch at the pool bar all alone. Time to Tami it up. I grabbed my wallet and pretended I was going into the hotel to buy a sandwich at the convenience shop. En route, I struck up a conversation with the man I had been trying to get access to the whole trip. In a playful voice, I said, "Excuse me. I think you're the guy who's been getting in the way of my business." He almost choked and said, "Excuse me?" I said, "Well, sure. You're the new global CMO of Bladi-blah. All of my contacts at your company are scared of you. I can't get them to commit to any future business. So, make a move already!" He laughed so hard. It turned into a piña colada-filled afternoon, and that lonely hotshot wound up becoming a BFF and an advisor to my future company.

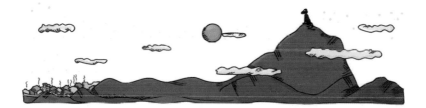

HIGH-LEVEL POSITIONS CAN BE ISOLATING.
NO ONE WANTS TO FEEL ALONE.
MAKE IT YOUR DUTY TO KEEP THE TOP DOGS COMPANY.

VALIDATION

Just as everyone feels vulnerable, so too they need to be seen, heard, and validated. It doesn't matter how important you think they are, or even how important they think they are. Everyone is saying to him or herself, "Did you see me? Did you hear me? Was I okay?"

★ The President of the United States cares what people think about his State of the Union address;

☆ Meryl Streep cares about her movie reviews; and

✳ Mark Zuckerberg cares if his friend request is denied.

By validating someone else, it shows you care, while also supplying him or her the feedback they need.

LET OTHERS KNOW THAT YOU HEAR THEM
AND THAT THEIR FEELINGS ARE VALID.

♡

DEGREES OF DYSFUNCTION

Whenever I try to find commonalities between people, usually because I am getting ready to introduce them to each other, the word "safe" comes to mind. We've talked a little bit about it in different contexts already. There are safe discussion topics (the weather), and then there's feeling safe. Huge difference. Feeling safe means you can talk to someone without worrying that you're being judged. As we get older, we realize that life is more interesting and rewarding when we aren't wasting time judging other people. We're all on our own paths, making our own decisions and discovering our own individual journey. And that journey is much better if it's shared, especially without the fear of judgment.

Our flaws are what make us unique and authentic. Let's not forget about the merits of being a 7 out of 10! Sharing your flaws, albeit uncomfortable for some, opens you up. Your vulnerability can be a strength. Some people run away from others when they open up, but I run toward them. If you're fucked up—fabulous! I am fucked up, too! How often have you heard someone say, "I have nothing in common with this person"? Well, guess what? You're both human and *we're all fucked up*, so start there. Sometimes when you realize other people are way more fucked up than you, it makes you feel fantastic, right? Don't lie. It does. It's okay. Everyone is dysfunctional; it's just a matter of degree.

One of the reasons I feel comfortable when I walk into a room is because I just assume everyone is more screwed up than me! Life is so much more layered and interesting when you understand we are all flawed. As my Aunt Gussie would say, "No one is perfect, no one has a halo on their head! 60% perfect is good enough." Since I am a "Perfect 7," I must be doing pretty good!

BE REALISTIC ABOUT WHO YOU ARE. AND REMEMBER, WE'RE ALL A LITTLE FUCKED UP, FABULOUS, AND FLAWED!

DIANE KEATON IS SEXY

"When I got older, I discovered gloves and hats and turtlenecks. When you get to a certain age, you shouldn't wear strapless gowns where everything is exposed because you look ridiculous. Just have fun. Smile. And keep putting on lipstick."
—DIANE KEATON

Have you read Diane Keaton's book, *Let's Just Say It Wasn't Pretty*? It's so refreshing to see how open she is about her insecurities. I was reading it on a plane, sitting in a window seat, on the way to meet a potential client. I was admiring her hysterical, self-deprecating humor and cracking up over her description of her "low-slung tits."

While deep in Diane's neuroses, the sun reflected my face on my tablet, and I could see every fine line (too many to count), every pore (in the millions), and my acne scars (which I will deal with just as soon as I can afford to take off for two consecutive weeks). I think Diane and Tami have something in common. I too, hide behind my glasses, love a good turtleneck, have never been married, and I see being neurotic as a way of life.

A date asked me once if I ever dress sexy. I was like, "What!?" I was dressed sexy on our date; I was wearing my favorite skintight Vivienne Westwood black pants and a low-cut shirt with a peek of cleavage, a white blazer, and high heels. Sexy is about attitude and how you feel about yourself, not about how much skin you show. I'm with Diane. My date turned out to be an asshole anyway. Don't fuck with me and fashion!

"STAY TRUE TO YOURSELF, EVEN IF YOU'RE AN ODDBALL."
(WE LOVE DIANE KEATON.)

VOICES In My HeAD

Whether I'm interviewing for a job or talking to a potential client, my internal dialogue is running incessantly. It's like having an alter ego. What is coming out of my mouth very rarely matches exactly what is churning in my head. The internal conversation reflects what I am truly feeling in the moment. It could be something funny, or it might tap into my insecurities, or it could even just be random shit, like what I am going to wear to the party tonight.

When I represented actors, my alter ego was constantly yammering things like this:

* Does she think I'm older than I am?
* Why is he putting all of his faith in me?
* Shit, I have more talent than they do.
* She thinks she's a lead? I see her more as the kooky best friend.
* Why is she is wearing an outfit that looks like the hooker scene from *Pretty Woman*?
* Should I wear the skirt or pants tonight?
* Crap, I have to pick up the dry cleaning.
* Did I lock the car?

Did it ever occur to you that everyone else is listening to the voices in their heads, too? Just imagine yourself having lunch with a client. Just two people can be the equivalent of up to six conversations.

1· The conversation you're having with your client;
2· The internal conversation in your head;
3· Your attempt to figure out your client's thoughts;
4 The conversation your client is having with you;
5· The internal conversation in your client's head; and
6· Your client's attempt to figure out what you're thinking.

Holy moly! This is maddening just thinking about it! How does anyone get anything done? Just imagine if there are six decision-makers in a room; that's 36 different conversations! We're lucky to close any deals!

YOUR ALTER EGO IS GIVING YOU SOME IMPORTANT MESSAGES (OR CONFUSING THE HELL OUT OF YOU). LISTEN TO YOUR DUELING THOUGHTS, BUT TRUST YOUR GUT.

IF ONLY I HAD A CRYSTAL BALL

How many times have you been stuck without an answer? In business it can be, why didn't I get the job? In your personal life it can be, why didn't he call me back? Whenever anyone (my associates, my girlfriends, my family) comes to me looking for answers, I always say, "I wish I had a crystal ball to take away your frustration."

We waste so much time (and in my case, money on therapy) trying to fill in the blanks and get answers. We need resolution, often, closure. Well, most of us aren't mind readers, so before you go bat-shit, straightjacket crazy, let's look at some options for moving forward.

I've tried some pretty ridiculous stuff out of sheer desperation for answers, such as:

★ Visiting a psychic;

★ Checking multiple horoscope sites;

☆ Throwing pennies in a fountain;

☀ Staring incessantly at my phone, waiting for something to happen;

★ Wishing on a stray eyelash;

☆ Mild stalking rituals; and

★ Non-subtle detective work.

More logical approaches might be to:

★ Build a foundation with your client so you can talk to them, ask for feedback, and make adjustments in the future;

☆ Understand that life is a probability game. When we win, we will be happy, and when we lose, we may have to be scraped off the floor; and

★ Find closure within yourself. It's a tough challenge, but gratifying. People rarely give us the answer we want to hear, anyway.

DON'T TORTURE YOURSELF BY PLAYING THE GUESSING GAME.
MOVE TOWARD THE FUTURE.

GENEVA

You will rarely hear me say a bad word about anyone. I am super nice to everyone, and I never want to rock the boat. My friends will attest to this because it drives some of them nuts. They nicknamed me "Geneva" accordingly. I have a lot of nicknames, as you may have gathered.

I despise conflict and avoid it at all costs, which was brought to my attention by an ex-boyfriend. He pointed out that disagreements can be healthy—the resolution can ultimately bring you closer together. He's right, and it makes perfect sense, but my neurotic side takes over because I hate it when people are upset with me. It totally freaks me out, and I lose sleep by overanalyzing the scenario to death! I know, you can't go through life without conflict; it's how you communicate and work to resolve it that matters.

As the European U.N. Headquarters and Red Cross home base, Geneva represents neutrality, peace, and respect for the human condition. For me, it's less of a Geneva complex (I can't give myself *that much* credit) and more about the ability to empathize. I value and respect each person's position in a conflict. In no way does that mean I don't get upset like everyone else, but I find it useful to put myself in the other person's shoes before I react. Being Geneva can piss people off. They want you to take a side. I might take a side eventually, but I'll still reflect on the opposing view.

───── ☾ ─────

SEE ALL SIDES BEFORE WEIGHING IN ON BUSINESS OR PERSONAL CONFLICTS (EVEN IF IT MEANS LOSING SLEEP OVER IT).

FIRST (AND LAST) IMPRESSIONS

"You will never get a second chance to make a first impression."
—WILL ROGERS

You only have one shot to make a good first impression, so pull your shit together and make sure you look good! This is something I like to think I've mastered. However, we must pay attention to both the first and the last impression we leave; they are equally important.

My Stepmother (who just happens to be a lot younger than my Father) got me off to an early start on the fashionista bandwagon. She had (and still does) a pretty fabulous closet, which she let me dip into freely. This began in the '80s when my friends and I hung out at the mall, and I rocked my Stepmother's parachute jumpsuit, cinched belt, and 4-inch espadrilles! I was well-trained to put a lot of effort into what looked good and what made me stand out, and I distinctly remember killing it back in the day. These days, looking good is still half the battle.

When I was just starting out, some clients wanted to party all night, and I definitely struggled to keep up. I was out with an associate one time who was having a blast, so I felt like I had to stay. I figured I could sweat it out for a couple more hours and be his wingman.

The next morning's conference sessions came quickly and, needless to say, I looked like a total train wreck. No, really. I was tired, hung over, and cold! (I'm always cold.) My Missoni knit scarf was wrapped around my neck and over my head like I was going skiing or had changed religions overnight. Out of the blue someone said, "Holy shit, I didn't recognize you!" (Because I looked homeless.)

Clients want you to hang out with them all night, but they still expect you to deliver in the morning. This is why, these days, I always sneak out before things get too crazy to get my eight hours of beauty-and-mental-clarity sleep. Back then, not only did I look awful that next day, I couldn't even string a sentence together.

So the moral of the story, folks: you only have one chance to make a first impression, but the last impression matters too, so make them both good. When you look good and put together, your clients respond favorably. Remember, you sell yourself first and your product second. The whole package needs to be zipped up and tight, kind of like my look in the '80s.

DON'T SHOW UP EXHAUSTED. IF IT'S THE LAST DAY OF AN EVENT, SKIP IT AND GO STRAIGHT TO THE AIRPORT!!!

"A bad dessert can ruin the meal."
—ANNE MCMANUS

TEE IT UP: NAIL THE PRE-SALE

By the time I get to the boardroom, the hardest part of my job is done. I have gathered the troops and teed up the sale. I am almost a spokesmodel at that point, smiling and nodding yes, yes, yes, with positivity!

If you are someone who naturally talks a lot (like me), this is the time to dial it down. Be quiet and turn on all of your senses. Listen to and read the room by paying attention, observing facial expressions, body language, and other cues. Your EQ is in full swing. Analyze the feedback. Sometimes the people we perceive to be the decision makers are not.

Use this time to channel the conversation if everyone is going off on tangents, and don't miss important opportunities. One of the most empowering moments is when you realize you've already succeeded just by being in the room. Use this strength to silently focus the discussion and direct the praise and credit to others.

FOCUS YOUR ENERGY ON LAYING THE GROUNDWORK.
BY THE TIME YOU'RE IN THE ROOM, YOUR WORK SHOULD BE DONE.

BOARDROOM BROAD

A CEO once told me there are only two types of people truly crucial in any company:

    1· Someone who makes something; and

    2· Someone who sells it.

Without someone making something, there's nothing to sell. Without someone to sell it, the thing rarely sells itself.

How to own the room like a boardroom broad:

* Show up on time. Being late is rude, and it also screams, "I don't respect your time." Your loss. Now you only have 45 minutes to bond with someone, as opposed to an hour;
* Treat the assistant like the CEO;
* Walk in the room with confidence. You're an influencer. Act like it;
* Be willing to take the lead and make introductions;
* Tee-up the meeting and set the tone;
* Let them know they can trust you to get shit done;
* Make them feel like they can't do the job without you.
* Don't check your phone. (Beyond rude);
* Pay attention to what they are saying. Let them speak without interruption;
* Don't furiously take notes in the meeting. You need to see the feedback in their faces;
* Don't leave the room until you've asked for the business;
* Laugh at even the dumbest jokes; and
* Follow up with a quick message to thank them for their time.

sells it

Your behavior and etiquette dictate
the future of the relationship.
Be a girl who knows better and own the room.

LEADERS INSPIRE

The first part of being a leader is to believe in yourself, what you're doing, and how it can help others succeed. Once you have a handle on those three elements, you can sell! When you are good to others, they want to work harder for you. Why not be likeable? True success as a leader is to inspire others to believe in you and get behind what you're doing. Inspiration leads to confidence, which leads to success, and the cycle goes on and on and on.

Simple Ways to Inspire:

- ★ Invite people to participate;
- ★ Be true to your word;
- ★ Exude optimism;
- ★ Be a role mode;
- ★ Care about people;
- ★ Share your failures, as much as your successes;
- ★ Acknowledge your imperfections;
- ★ Be an advocate for people, encourage their potential;
- ★ Paint a picture with stories and examples;
- ★ Build up others' sense of worth;
- ★ Tell people you are proud of them when they do something good; and
- ★ Be consistent.

INSPIRE OTHERS TO SUCCEED;
IT WILL SHINE BACK ON YOU.

BE CONSISTENT

Being consistent is one of the most important leadership qualities that exist. If people can't trust you to show up to a meeting, what does that say about how you will treat their business? Life outside work is challenging and unpredictable enough; when it comes to choosing partners in business, we want people we can count on. We want to surround ourselves with people who do what they say they will do.

Have you ever noticed when you cancel a meeting, it seems to give the other person a free pass to cancel on you? If you're unreliable, it suggests that you're not consistent, either. You need to be true to your word with actions. People will only allow you so many chances to demonstrate that you value their time as much as your own.

Inconsistent personality types create their own set of problems. They're sometimes moody and you don't know who you are going to get (the devil or the angel) at any given moment, which makes for a pretty shitty work environment. It also causes a chain reaction, because you're not the only one who has to keep the devil at bay. Everyone in their path, including clients, is subject to their unpredictable behavior.

Trust is built on consistency; your character is something you can control!

BE A PERSON OTHERS CAN RELY ON.

DON'T BORE THE BUYER

"You've got to find the fun in everything."
—JOHN LEGERE, CEO OF T-MOBILE

My reputation in business is solid. People have come to expect the process will be easier, more successful and, most importantly, more fun if I am involved. I must not disappoint, so the last thing I can afford to do when we get in the room is show up with a bunch of other people who bore the pants off the buyers.

The real reason for a face-to-face meeting is to gauge the team's approach and to get a sense of their personalities and capabilities. If I have done my job correctly, they have already bought into what we're selling. The way we can secure the business is by being connected, engaged, and likable.

There have been times I have prepped my team thoroughly and, when we get in the room, they still act like a pack of robots—doing what they think is safe, professional, and expected. They might even show that same effing presentation the client has seen time and time again. PowerPoint, PowerPoint, PowerPoint. Ugh. I am already bored just thinking about it. Dry presentations and lengthy materials were boring in school, right? Well, guess what? They're STILL boring.

Nothing will kill the meeting quicker than cluttered slides with mini-point font. It's comparable to a hot, overcrowded elevator that stops on every floor. As soon as someone squints during your presentation, you're fucked. I've witnessed firsthand, an entire boardroom get lost in a sea of words and graphs. Let's have a stimulating conversation with our potential partners.

An associate once asked me, "Why do you think our competitor is always winning over us?" My knee-jerk response was, "Because they are cooler." This was probably not the most constructive feedback, but it was the truth.

I knew from being out in the marketplace that the competitor's materials were amazing: action-packed videos depicting their capabilities through visuals and other creative means. They were not boring the client with the eight-point font PowerPoint presentation; they were wowing them in 3D interactive.

Second, the competitor's people were approachable. The CEO was accessible; the whole team was dressed in hip, business-casual attire, and they instantly made you feel comfortable. Every aspect of their business—from their appearance to their approach to the science and body of their work—sent a consistent message: this is a partnership you want to be a part of.

Take off the cheap suit and give people digestible information, preferably visuals, and a short, sexy video. Your pitch deck should be ten pages or fewer, using a large font, and it should contain pertinent information only. You can attach an appendix with lots of back-up details. Do not overcomplicate it. Remember, overloading the audience doesn't equal a better presentation. You should be able to finish the pitch in 20 minutes total. Most meetings are set in hour blocks, so you want enough time to shoot the shit and deliver your pitch with ease.

Once you leave, you should be working on next steps, and the golden opportunity is sitting on a serving platter ready for the taking.

Keep these five simple things in mind:

1. Be passionate;
2. Be inspiring;
3. Be brief;
4. Be captivating; and
5. Be clear.

If you can't avoid the PowerPoint and if you must deliver a presentation, here is an ideal sequence.

Shoot the shit: 10 minutes. Wait for any important late arrivals, keep it personal, and light—something you can draw on for bonding or follow-up.

Open forum: 15 minutes. Ask if there are specific questions or concerns they would like addressed. Stall, if waiting for the decision-maker.

Make the pitch: 15-20 minutes. Focus on high-level bullet points that allow you to expand so you aren't reading word-for-word from slides.

Make the ask: One minute. For the love of God, ask for the business.

Allow Q & A: 10 minutes. Self-explanatory.

Make the close: Five minutes. Clear next steps on moving forward with the business.

*"People who know what they're talking about
don't need PowerPoint."*
— STEVE JOBS

IN THE IMMORTAL WORDS OF ADVERTISING GIANT OGILVY & MATHER, "YOU CANNOT BORE PEOPLE INTO BUYING YOUR PRODUCT; YOU CAN ONLY INTEREST THEM IN BUYING IT."

SPHINCTER³⁸-THE PERFECT EMAIL FOLLOW-UP

Your communication outside the boardroom is important, too. My emails are always short and sweet, straight and to the point, but not rough around the edges. If I've met the person, I like to throw in a little humor, especially if we had a good connection, and I can refer to something clever that we bonded over. If you don't know the person, and you're trying to connect for the first time, keep your correspondence light, casual, and conclude with a general "we should compare notes" statement. Do the heavy lifting on the phone or in person.

When communicating by email or text, I tend to use a lot of exclamation points, which I know is not advised, but it works for me!! It's difficult to convey my enthusiasm otherwise, and I want to expose my personality as soon as possible. (By the way, I received an email littered with exclamation points from a very high-level male CEO; so don't believe for a hot second it's just us girls who do that.)

I am always looking for a chance to enhance the overall energy right from the jump, and exclamation points get the job done. Will Schwalbe, author of the book, *Send: Why People Email So Badly and How to Do It Better*, says, "Email has such a flattening effect: it's toneless and affectless. The exclamation point is the quickest and easiest way to kick things up a notch, but not if you're angry. Only happy exclamation points."

---

38 Sphincter: ring-like muscle found in the anus
   (http://www.urbandictionary.com/define.php?term=sphincter)

Sample correspondence with a CEO and founder:

→ *Hi Gary,*
Great meeting you! I am the one who is friends with Brooke. You are talented, funny, brilliant and have a gorgeous supportive family, but the fact you said "sphincter" on stage, completely put you over the edge to be my new favorite person! Let's stay in touch!

↳ *Hello, Tami!*
Thanks so much for the kind words! The last thing on my bucket list was to be able to call out the Pulaski Skyway as the armpit of the sphincter of New Jersey on a stage before an audience of seasoned marketers. I'm all done now. That's it for me. ;) Please send Brooke my best if you chat with her before I do (she's one of my fav peeps, and I never get to see her!!!), and yes, let's keep in touch for sure!!!

→ *Gary,*
Being yourself and having fun is the best marketing. It builds trust and loyalty and you nailed it!!! I will see Brooke next week. You can count on me to send her a message, and I will even throw in a hug!
Take it easy!
Tami

↳ *Thanks, Tami!*
Rock on!!!
Gary

BE CLEVER, KEEP IT SHORT, AND HAVE FUN
WHEN FOLLOWING UP WITH CLIENTS.

CUSS WITH CLASS

You are fucking brilliant! Who doesn't want to be fucking brilliant? It sure sounds better than being smart. I do swear a lot, but when I cuss, I cuss with class. To me, dropping the occasional F-bomb gets the point across. Swearing and exclamation points—I'm all in!

So many times, after a business meeting, the smarty-pants associates have said to me, "You know, that guy is really cool. He used the F-bomb." People put on different hats on at work. I get it; we all do. But when someone drops the F-bomb, you can breathe a sigh of relief knowing you can be yourself. I was once described as a rainmaker with a potty mouth—I loved it!

In Timothy Jay's and Kristin Janschewitz's report, "The Science of Swearing," everyday English speakers swear in 0.5% of his or her daily words. While swearing occurs most in Type A personalities, the women dominate in the frequency of public swearing. Way to fucking go, girls!

According to Dr. Richard Stephens, who is a senior lecturer from Keele University, "The stereotype that those who swear have a low IQ or are inarticulate is wrong. It is rich emotional language." Not to mention the fact swearing relieves pain, according to Dr. Stephens. So fucking swear all you want—it's good for you!

It works, people!

 SHOW YOU ARE HEALTHY, ENTHUSIASTIC AND APPROACHABLE BY CUSSING WITH CLASS!

"At 70 years old, if I could give my younger self one piece of advise, it would be to use the word "Fuck Off" much more frequently."

— HELEN MIRREN

THE PEPSI CHALLENGE: CORPORATE FLAIR

I was getting dressed for a big meeting with Pepsi and digging around in my closet for something to wear that would let me stand out and be memorable. I spotted my vintage Pepsi belt, which had been gifted to me a few years back as part of a VIP swag bag at a party. It's a fantastic belt, and I used to wear it all the time. I figured why not? I paired it with a sharp, fitted, "you wish you had my body" chocolate pinstripe suit, mustard top, and heels that jacked me up to 6'1". This big Pepsi logo belt was impossible to ignore, but when I arrived at the meeting, no one said ANYTHING.

Shit. My internal fashion police started balking. "You are such a dork. You look so effing lame right now. You way overplayed it this time, Tami!" Okay, I thought, I'll just accept it. I'm a geek. I tried to get over it and pay attention. The meeting was supposed to be two hours long, we were already 90 minutes into discussions, and the head of the division hadn't even shown up yet. We had a dinner scheduled immediately following the meeting, so I was facing a never-ending fashion faux pas torture.

As I suffered through the remaining minutes and hours of my dorkiness, in walked the man of the hour for a quick appearance. I stood up to introduce myself, towering over every man in the room. He shook my hand, looked me over from head to toe . . . paused . . . and said, "nice belt." I wanted to die. But, it was *the moment*. At dinner, he paraded me around to everyone in the room, pointing at my belt and saying, "She is so cool to have the balls to wear a friggin' logo'd belt to the meeting."

TAKE CHANCES! IF IT DOESN'T WORK OUT, WHO GIVES A FUCK?

PACKING RITUALS

Packing for a business trip is friggin' hard! I want outfit options when I travel, so being limited to one carry-on bag is a serious challenge. For me, packing is a ritual. If time permits, I'll take three days to strategize my looks. From time to time, I establish a theme. My most recent business trip was framed by a Ralph Lauren casual chic style; an English riding look complete with ruffled blouses, tailored riding jackets, and riding boots.

You need to pull off the right combo of something sexy with something conservative. For example, if you are wearing a short skirt, pair it with a loose or flowy top. Wear skinny jeans with something elegant. Fit, however, is the most important consideration. Your clothes must be tailored and flattering.

Lastly, age appropriate dress is a MUST. Don't be tempted to wear your hoochie skirt just because it fits. Dressing younger than you are makes you look like you're trying too hard, which is not a good look.

A smart approach to packing is to have some quality staple pieces you know are winners. Statement accessories are also a key ingredient. I always bring a few of my favorite scarves and throw one on to change up an outfit.

The way you dress gives off context clues about your energy, mood, and personality. Your appearance sends a message to those around you, such as, "I did not bother to get dressed up because I don't really care about the outcome of this meeting." Or, if you're not properly dressed for the occasion (think ball gown at a barbeque), your confidence will be affected because you'll be hyperaware of your mistake. Do your research about the event you're attending and always try your outfits on before you pack them.

When our casual, hip startup was acquired by a much more

conservative corporate entity, the "suits" infiltrated the office. Our clients noticed immediately. They said, "You guys have gotten pretty stiff, eh? Everyone is so buttoned up around here." We became less approachable and it's one of the main reasons we lost their business. Funny (and not funny), but true.

DEVELOP PACKING RITUALS. YOUR CHOICE OF CLOTHING MATTERS; IT GIVES CLUES TO OTHERS ABOUT YOUR PERSONALITY.

BEFRIEND THE "ENEMY"

It may sound crazy, but it's not cheating if you help your competitors. They're your peers, you're all in the same boat and they understand business development is about relationships. Some of the best referrals I've received are from my "competition." Sometimes, we even team up at events and compliment each other's capabilities.

If your competition is helping to build a successful industry offering, your business will benefit, too. You know the trials and tribulations each other face, and you can share insights and best practices to succeed. Plus, you never know when you might switch companies, and your competition will become your coworkers. Trust and respect will already be built in!

If there is direct business at hand, we'll all get a chance to throw our hat in the ring. Often, one company simply has a more appropriate skill set than the other. If that's the case and your competitor is better-suited, then by all means, they should get the business. Further, you should acknowledge that fact. It's honest, decent, and it's what's best for that client. You'll be setting a precedent on how you do business with both competitors and potential clients. I know my relationships will always consult with me first and they know I'll refer them to a competitor if it's in their best interest.

At times, competition can strengthen your core business, and to enhance the strength of your personal network, the competition should be treated as associates.

 THERE IS ENOUGH WORK FOR EVERYONE.
MAKE FRIENDS WITH YOUR COMPETITORS.
THEY ARE YOUR ALLIES, NOT YOUR ENEMIES.

THE HOLZMAN HUNT

A couple of years ago, my co-workers asked me to speak about new business development and strategy at our annual marketing summit. Knowing my sense of humor, they had a massive slide created that depicted me, hunting my prey with a spear. The image hung behind me as I presented and compelled me to entertain the crowd with a stand-up routine full of self-deprecating jokes and a lot of energy.

I hammed it up big time and gave them examples of what I do at conferences to get people's attention: buy them a drink, hold court, tell them a dirty joke, the usual stuff. Even though I was in front of a large group of professionals, I didn't hold anything back and reinforced the idea you need big balls or a tough vajayjay to walk up to people in this business. I was 100% authentic and the feedback I received validated the effectiveness of that approach. We had been analyzing reports all day and we were thirsty for something sassy and engaging.

It's been years since I shared my secret sauce and the Holzman Hunt success stories with that executive team, but they all still talk about it. The company founder said, "Holy shit, Tami, you pumped up that room, made us all laugh and have fun. There was renewed energy and a new moment of inspiration."

Nothing I said was scientific or based on marketing strategy research; that's for fucking sure. But I inspired those in my company and they bought what I was selling, which was to remind them why they were paying me the big bucks—to connect with the C-suite like no one else in that room could even dream.

DON'T FORGET TO INSPIRE AND
REMIND YOUR INTERNAL TEAM WHY THEY HIRED YOU.

CHAPTER 12

PERCEPTION IS REALITY

THE IT FACTOR

What makes you stand out? The "It Factor" is not a single attribute one is born with or acquires over time. On the contrary, it's more of an equation specific to each individual. It's that "Je ne sais quoi" you can't quite put your finger on.

Your strengths, interests, quirks, drive, compassion, and motivation, combined with self-confidence, produces your unique It Factor. When you have "It," you naturally radiate self-assurance in an almost hypnotic way. Like bears to honey. You aren't the fuel to the flame, but the spark that creates the first flicker.

Have you ever been so drawn to a speaker their very presence awakens you? Do you perk up and immerse yourself in their every word? That's the It Factor. Someone else could say the same exact thing and make you feel as if there was a carbon monoxide leak in the room.

Everyone has the potential to utilize their unique It Factor, but it requires fearless and honest self-discovery and acceptance. It's inside all of us; we just have to figure out how to unlock it, nurture it, and use it to our advantage. Learn to recognize the It Factor in yourself and others. It's attitude, charisma, and demeanor—not looks (but that helps). Go toward the people that mesmerize you.

Working with actors was an excellent way for me to dissect this elusive and attractive quality. I knew within seconds who had It and who didn't. It came down to owning every part of their personalities: the good, the bad, and the ugly. That level of self-acceptance is the catalyst to enviable self-confidence we should all strive to gain.

A couple of years ago, I was at the ESPY awards with a group of guys. Across the room the boys spotted the biggest heartthrob for every woman over 40: the plumber from *Desperate Housewives*!

Now you would think I was the one freaking out, but it was the guys who were wetting themselves trying to get a picture with him to send to their own desperate wives. My male posse persuaded me to approach him for a photo op and he kindly accepted.

What followed next surprised me. Mike Delfino, in the flesh said, "Can I get a photo with you?" I looked at him with a puzzled expression and he asked again, "Can I get a photo with you?" Who am I to argue with TV's biggest heartthrob at the time? Of course I agreed to a romantic photo of the two of us. We started talking and he told me that everyone at the bar was trying to figure out who I was. At this point, I was thinking that the waiters had put something in the drinks and everyone was hallucinating on acid. But you know what? Mike Delfino wasn't crazy. That night, I was someone—I was the "IT Girl!"

ABOVE ALL ELSE, BE CONFIDENT AND COMFORTABLE IN YOUR OWN SKIN, NO MATTER WHERE YOU ARE OR WHO YOU ARE TALKING TO.

IDA: INTERNET DISCRETION ADVISED

Social media allows you to market yourself as an entire brand with an infinite reach. It's a limitless and incredible tool if you use it wisely. When I troll social networking sites, I cringe when I read some of my associates' posts. You must be very careful with your opinions, personal beliefs, values, and activity. Over-sharing is simply not smart—when in doubt, don't post.

Social networking gives you the advantage of looking behind the curtain into your clients' personal lives. It's a cheat sheet for talking points. Using this information appropriately will help you to build relationships more quickly. It's also an amazing tool if you're a bit shy and find it difficult to walk right up to people in person.

First: your photo. For God's sake, use the hottest picture you have and if you're dissatisfied with your library, make sure it's, at least, interesting. Photoshop it if you must, add a unicorn in the background, whatever. Understand, people are going to look at it, and it will make a first impression. That's life. Recently I wanted to change my profile picture, so I recruited five friends to help me. I told them I wanted it to be pretty, sophisticated, approachable, sexy, and sweet. There was a unanimous vote, and I am happy with our choice.

Try to maintain a little mystery and keep'em interested. It's more exciting to read posts from someone who shares less frequently than "that guy" hogging up the newsfeed plugging something new every chance he gets. If you dilute yourself as a brand, you risk losing the interest of your followers.

Pay close attention to what others post and, if you're turned off by it, stay away from the same patterns. You would be surprised how quickly you can get sucked into the social media vortex of inappropriate posting.

Be smart with privacy. I've changed my settings, so I approve (or disapprove) anytime someone wants to tag me in a post or a picture. It's much safer that way. Never assume others will use the same discretion as you.

Don't limit yourself to just "liking" a post. Comment on pictures of people's kids or give them props for a recent achievement. If someone had a baby, raised money for a charity, or got a promotion, that's your opportunity to stand out from the pack and send him or her a note, make a donation, call, or even send a small gift to congratulate them. (Review your company's gift giving policies. You don't want to get fired for trying to be nice!)

Also, take advantage of the fact that you can see when you're in the same city at the same time as one of your connections. It's easier to plan meetings with muckety-mucks when you are both out of your respective environments.

Keep in mind how quickly things can be misinterpreted via social media, texts, and even email. For example, in my best valley girl speak, I used to say, "Shut up!" as in, "No way, get out of town!" but someone actually thought I was telling them to shut up and it wasn't well-received. Always consider how others may interpret your intention and modify messages if there's a chance it could be misconstrued.

People talk. People listen. They always have, but today, it spreads like wildfire. It's amazing how quickly news travel about something negative.

 DRINKING AND POSTING CAN BE HAZARDOUS. THINK BEFORE YOU POST.

SOCIAL MEDIA DO'S AND DON'TS:

▷ Don't say how old you are ☺ . It's irrelevant;

▷ Don't share pictures of you reliving your drunken college youth;

▷ Under no circumstances should you go on a political rant. You will alienate a potential client;

▷ Don't be vague; it's annoying: i.e., "Having a really bad day..." You look like an attention-seeker and a Debbie Downer;

▷ Don't post meaningless messages. There should be a point to each post;

⇨ No one cares about your dentist appointment;

⇨ Don't ever show your bitter side. Use your social sites as a way to highlight a positive. Keep the negative pity party for the therapist's office;

☆ Do promote something that is worth communicating;

☆ Do share photos of your family, but without overkill;

☆ Do share your charitable causes and participate in others;

☆ Do recognize when someone accomplishes something;

☆ Do share and celebrate other people's successes;

☆ Do brag a little; don't make it a habit;

★ Do occasionally post something funny or inspirational; and

☆ Do recruit your friends for feedback before sharing an important post.

GET YOUR BEAUTY SLEEP!

"Sleep Your Way to the Top"[39] is an amazing article written by Arianna Huffington. I wish I could just "schtoop"[40] my way to the top but unfortunately, that's not the way it works, nor was it her message. I couldn't agree more with Arianna about how important it is to get a good night's sleep. It not only makes you think more clearly, but you look better, too. I am convinced there are fewer wrinkles after a solid eight because once I see the wrinkles in the morning, I pretty much see them all day. The more I try to cover them, the more my makeup gets stuck in the cracks. I am positive getting enough sleep helps keep me out of the insane asylum.

Simply getting enough sleep can enhance creativity, ingenuity, confidence, leadership, and decision-making skills. "Sleep deprivation negatively impacts our mood, our ability to focus, and our ability to access higher level cognitive functions: the combination of these factors is what we generally refer to as mental performance," say Drs. Stuart Quan and Russell Sanna, from Harvard Medical School's Division of Sleep Medicine.

---

39 http://www.inc.com/arianna-huffington/sleep-your-way-to-the-top.html

40 **Schtoop:** To fuck. Can mean anything from 'fucking' or 'to fuck,' but is becoming just an exclamatory word (such as, in place of saying 'Wow!' or 'Oh my!'). Also used in place of 'cool' or when there just isn't anything better so say, and you want a conversation to end. Usually pronounced in a very long and drawn out way. (http://www.urbandictionary.com/define.php?term=schtoop)

My Jewish mother told me to add exercise to this section because that also helps with your mental state and makes you get a good night sleep. How guilty do I feel right now with my skinny ass on the couch?

BEAUTY SLEEP IS NOT A MYTH, AND THAT GOES FOR MEN TOO!

HOT CEO, HUGE IPO

It totally sucks the big one that looks matter; I really wish this weren't the case, even though (and because) I do put a good amount of effort into how I look and, even though I know it's superficial (and exhausting trying to keep up!), just another reason I need my beauty sleep. Beauty has been embedded in our brains and culture as a measure of success. Why do you think presidential candidates hire stylists, get Botox, and endure media training? They get the glam squad and the media training, so they look good on camera!

Two economists from the University of Wisconsin conducted a study on how looks impact monetary value in a business setting. Joseph T. Halford and Hung-Chia Hsu, in "Beauty is Wealth: CEO Appearance and Shareholder Value," say:

> *CEOs with a higher Facial Attractiveness Index are associated with better stock returns, higher returns upon acquisition announcements and higher total compensation. This finding confirms the existence of the "beauty premium" in CEO pay.*

They stress that making a good first impression pays the big bucks, a beauty premium. They use a Facial Attractive Index to measure symmetry (because they are economists and not Hollywood agents). As you know from the Facial Attractive Analysis I shared in Chapter 1, my score was only 7 out of 10 because my nose is too long for my ears. I can't help but laugh. I may have to get the nose job after all, and I may get a raise!

Politicians and CEOs know—appearances do matter.

LOOKING SMART, FEELING FUCKING BRILLIANT

I wear glasses, which most people view as a sign of being smart, so many give me extra credit for being intelligent. This is a perfect example of how people buy into perception. When my glasses are on, POOF, a miracle, suddenly I'm the smart chick in the room. Forget about it! The reality is, I am just handicapped. (Fuck, why the hell was I cheating off of kids with glasses back in high school? Not my highest EQ moment!)

Glasses have become both a crutch and a signature look. I have multiple pairs I get to hide behind. There was a time when I only wore a pair of pink Prada glasses. People stopped me constantly to compliment them. I tried to replace them at one point with an, even more, expensive red pair, but there was something about the pink, something that was so different and so hard for others to pull off. When they broke, I literally had a panic attack. I was like Linus without his blanket or Batman without his cape. Told you I'm neurotic!

My glasses are my secret weapon. Not only do they help me see, but they help others see me in a sexy librarian light, or as David Lee Roth of Van Halen said, "Too Hot for Teacher!"

WEAR SOMETHING THAT MAKES YOU FEEL BRILLIANT AND POWERFUL, I.E. DESIGNER GLASSES, ITALIAN POWER SUIT, YVES SAINT LAURENT BRIEFCASE.

THE PROOF IS IN THE PUDDING

A while ago, I was having lunch and catching up with the COO of one of the top three global media companies. It turned out he wanted to hire someone who had excellent relationships with C-level executives. Their old way of selling TV advertising was becoming stale and he was looking for new contacts. I was like, "Hello! I have amazing relationships. This is what I do!" I said, "Who are you having lunch with?" He was confused and looked around the restaurant. I asked again, "Who are you having lunch with?" He was still not getting it and said, "You. I'm having lunch with you, Tami." I said, "Right. See? I can get lunch with anyone! Even you!" I didn't wind up working for him, but he got the point.

There are only so many chances to get a meeting based on your relationships, and those relationships pay the bills. My business development currency is my Rolodex. In theory, my connections are my own version of a Harvard degree. If you should ever end ties with your current company (which will happen at some point), you'll always have your kickass Rolodex to fall back on.

Relationship-building is a skill set that crosses all industries and departments. Use it to your advantage.

IF YOU CAN HAVE LUNCH WITH A TOP EXECUTIVE, THEN YOU CAN HAVE LUNCH WITH ANYONE.

AN INFLUENCER? YES!

Probably the best compliment I've ever received was when someone referred to me as an influencer. The first time I heard someone call me that, I thought, "Really, ME?" I looked around to see if someone uber-fabulous was standing behind me, but nope, it was just me, the "Perfect 7," influencing others. I'll never forget the first time I was asked to wear a product because, they told me, "You will influence the right crowd to buy it." I was like, "Holy shit, I've arrived, I'm a business development celebrity."

The network I've been able to build is a strong factor as to why one might see me as an influencer. Developing connections is not something you can study; it's an investment of time into people over profit. Without an agenda, I put myself out there and gain the confidence needed to establish these connections, which allows me to be an influencer by association. You can brand yourself, and you can meet a million people but, if there's no connection, your brand has no value, and your relationships aren't real.

Remember, when you find yourself in a boardroom filled with hugely successful executives, they're people, too. Don't question yourself if you disagree with what they're saying or have something to add. People will come to expect this from you; don't disappoint.

AN INFLUENCER IS ONLY AS STRONG
AS HIS OR HER CONNECTIONS.

FROM "PLUS ONE" TO POTUS (AND BEYOND)

"To those of you who received honors, awards and distinctions,
I say well done. And to the C-students, I say you, too, can be
President of the United States." [41]

—GEORGE W. BUSH

I am beyond grateful that I'm often invited to inner circles, but how did I get there? One VIP leads to another, and it all comes down to perception. People make assumptions about your success based on who you surround yourself with. If you're at an exclusive party, you have instant access to the power players in the room (whether you were invited or you crashed).

I was invited as a "plus one" to an intimate fundraiser luncheon with the President of the United States, and I couldn't say yes fast enough! Who wouldn't want to have lunch with the POTUS and be among the wealthiest businessmen and women in the country, all gathered together in one room? And guess what? By association, I was seen as a wealthy successful businesswoman, too! Who cares what your political beliefs are! There I was, the perpetual C-student, getting ready to shake hands with a fellow C-student (yes, I'm talking about George W. Bush)—the CEO of the nation and the Commander-in-Chief of the Armed Forces. The C-Suite doesn't get any higher than that, people!

By a completely random act of chance, I had been at a cocktail party in the same home where the POTUS lunch was. I always bring a hostess gift, and I had given the woman who hosted the cocktail party (and the POTUS lunch) a box of beautiful little soaps.

---

41 http://www.usatoday.com/story/news/nation-now/2015/05/17/george-w-bush-c-students-president-graduation/27488795/

Then, on the day of the POTUS luncheon, I noticed MY SOAPS were in every bathroom. OMG! Talk about the Presidential Seal of Approval for my tastes in a hostess gift! Back to Ross Dress for Less to buy more soaps! But I digress…

As you might imagine, the room was buzzing with excitement that day. Even the most high-level power players get their knickers in a twist over the POTUS! My date and I had the good fortune of being seated near Meg Whitman (CEO of Hewlett-Packard, duh). I was an entrepreneur at the time, and my date suggested I share what my company was doing with her. I took his advice and went for it, and holy shit, Meg Whitman loved my idea! She said it reminded her of why she had gone to work for eBay; she even invited us to have lunch with her in San Jose. Being in the room with all of the other wildly successful people gave me instant credibility, and she also genuinely loved my idea. What a day! I was on top of the world with the Pres.

PERCEPTION IS REALITY.

CHAPTER 13

THE DOUCHEBAG THEORY: KNOW WHO YOU ARE DEALING WITH

CUT THE BULLSHIT

Everyone likes the "no bullshit" person. How many times have you heard someone say, "How refreshing! That guy is no B.S." It's kind of sad that the ultimate compliment is not to be full of shit! Always take the no B.S. approach and be genuine in your endeavors—in both positive and negative situations. Phony and disingenuous compliments and/or apologies are worse than silence.

NO BULLSHIT—being authentic is in! Of course, there are times when we're given an advanced-level job or high-pressure meeting and we may not feel 100% capable of pulling it off. If you don't know an answer or if you don't have the solution, just come clean and say you'll bring in the right people who do know. Being honest about what I don't know has gotten me a lot further than when I've tried to fake it. I don't fake it in sex or business, and that has brought me great success... and orgasms. Not necessarily in that order.

I have positioned myself as a high-level business lead generator. My colleagues expect me to connect decision makers. They know this is where my talent lies and, more importantly, that I will continue to take care of them and help them along the way. I can be trusted to follow through, and people know what to expect from me: I deliver. Develop what you're good at and surround yourself with experts in other areas.

PEOPLE CAN SMELL BULLSHIT — BE AUTHENTIC.

THE VICTIM CARD

People who play the victim card are angry. (No shit, Sherlock.) Often, their attitude is rooted in negativity, and they blame external factors (including their associates). This generally leads to some ugly passive-aggressive behavior. They desperately try to protect themselves and their fragile egos while crapping on everyone around them.

Sadly, I've seen people use the victim card to try to get ahead, which is appalling. They point the finger at everyone else for their misery or failure and cry, "Poor me! I'm an innocent victim!" They have an excuse for everything and it's never ever their fault. There are too many schmucks like me out there who try to "save" people and make it right for them and wind up getting manipulated in the process.

Sorry to use a cliché, but misery does love company. Have you noticed that there is a cult of unhappy people? Bad energy spreads like a disease—even I get wrapped up in the shit-talking. This is the Putz Negative Currency Model at work! Even if you have the ability to look at the situation or person logically and say to yourself, "I'm getting sucked into this person's misery, and it's bringing me down," do not let toxic people control you. The more effort we put toward staying in our happy space, the more likely we are to take the power away from the negative victims.

Don't get me wrong—of course there are people who just plain have bad luck. There are legitimate situations where pain and misery are justified, even expected, which is an entirely different matter.

I wish we could be allocated a certain number of complaint days in a year, but let's keep it under 365. ☺

Don't play into victims, because you're not doing them any favors.

THE DOUCHEBAG THEORY

"It's nothing personal; it's just business." Who came up with this cop-out theory? Just saying, but it had to be a total douchebag. (This might be one of my favorite words. It's so accurate.).

We spend more time working than we do in our personal lives. We build real relationships with our associates and customers. If you don't feel a personal disappointment when a client fires you or you lose a $30M deal, I'm sorry, but you're not normal.

When I received an email from a client saying he wanted to terminate our relationship because we were difficult to work with and inflexible as a partner, my stomach dropped. I was nauseated to learn someone was so disappointed in our relationship, that they were firing us! Despite being assured this decision wasn't directed at me, of course, I felt personally responsible. Which is normal, by the way; that's how you should feel. You shouldn't blow it off and say, "Fuck it; it's business, and if they don't like it, they can go somewhere else." Business can be cutthroat, but that mentality is detrimental to everyone.

No one wants to work with douchebags. My clients want to be heard and they want their business partners to have compassion. "It's nothing personal; it's just business" is dated. Gone are the days when our work and our personal lives could be completely separate.

When Blankety Blank acquired the small, start-up tech company I was working for, I thought it was a good time to introduce my BFF (business friend forever), an executive at a Fortune 500 company, to our new team. The goal was to educate the team on the acquisition and how it had expanded our reach and overall capabilities. This was also a perfect time to win the business that we hadn't been able to secure as a smaller company. It should have been a shoo-in. Unfortunately, I was not prepared for how my new boss would behave. He decided to play devil's advocate on virtually everything the Fortune 500 executive had to say. Not only did he challenge her ruthlessly, but he also created an uncomfortable situation for everyone involved. Our goal is not to question or second-guess our clients, but to offer them better solutions and customized options that fit their business needs. Needless to say, we didn't get the business.

That disaster reminds me of another time when an old boss told me while pointing his finger in my face, "You know what your problem is? You don't know how to handle rejection when a client doesn't want to work with us." I looked around to see who he was talking to. There was no way it could be me! The inner voice in my head said, "Excuse me," as I got the wax out of my ear. "I think you are insulting me, but I also hear a compliment in there. *I don't see the rejection.* I am 100% confident that this client will work with me. This company had been a preferred client for years, with millions of dollars in business. I am sorry they don't share the same enthusiasm for meeting with you. Maybe if you didn't take a know-it-all approach, the deal would have worked out differently." In reality, I sat there dumbfounded at his comment, with my jaw on the ground. It happened to be *his ego* that was getting in the way of our growing the relationship with this client.

If you don't take it personally when it comes to business, it's a sign that you are only in business for yourself and that you don't care about the client relationship (which makes you a douchebag). We've all seen our fair share of selfish and shortsighted behavior. Of course, there are times when people don't see eye to eye. Unfortunately, instead of everyone taking a minute to look into him or herself and see if there is a way to mend or change the dynamic, people tend to ignore their behavior because their ego is getting in the way. In addition to this being insanely narrow minded, it has a trickle-down effect on the team. A douchebag tends to find fault in everything, versus looking at the positives. How much better would a little positivity impact the team? Think about it.

ADDITIONAL DB BEHAVIOR:

- Putting the competition down, which puts your client in an awkward position. (Just highlight your strengths and keep your opinions to yourself);

- Challenging your clients in meetings, playing devil's advocate;

- Being a know-it-all;

- Being a name dropper;

- Being a gossip; or

- Being a narcissist.

DON'T BE A DOUCHEBAG.
THE COOLER THE PERSON, THE MORE ATTRACTIVE THEY BECOME.
OR, IF THEY'RE A TOOL, THE LESS ATTRACTIVE THEY BECOME.

BAD ADVICE

I met this young guy (probably 23 or so) at a business cocktail party. We exchanged the usual pleasantries, and he told me he worked for one of the major consumer product companies. I said, "Cool, where's your badge?" He told me that Joe Blow (who happened to be a business development executive I know) gave him some great advice: "He told me not to wear my badge because everyone would be bothering me and pitching me their business." WHAT?

I said, "That is the worst advice I have ever heard. Your job is to meet people and connect with them and find the next big thing. You're here to meet people you can do business with. How many times in your life will people want to talk to you and approach you because you have a powerful position, and they need something from you?"

Out of pure annoyance with Joe Blow (douchebag) and his stupid, terrible advice, I continued to freak out on the kid and said, "Listen, I'm going to act as your big sister because you need one right now:

1. Go put your badge back on;
2. Meet as many people as you can; and
3. Remember, anyone here could end up hiring you later or be your business partner down the road.

At 23, you don't know where life will take you. Don't foreclose the possibility of meeting and connecting with people just because some business development loser told you not to wear your badge. If anything, you want your name out there. You want to be heard, and you want to be known. Just for the record, I am really close to your boss's boss. Do you realize that by not wearing your badge, you are going to lose out on the opportunity for me to go back and tell him that I met you? Already, we're looking at a major potential lost opportunity for you to get ahead in your own company—all because you are taking advice from Joe Blow. He doesn't get it."

The kid put his badge on.

MEET AS MANY PEOPLE AS POSSIBLE,
WHICHEVER SIDE OF THE TABLE YOU ARE ON.

YOU, ME. LAYOVER IN BOISE?

The key to preserving your sanity is to have enough clients that you are not forced to work with people you don't like. If you're in a desperate situation and have bills and staff to pay, you may start to compromise your standards. Try to avoid the dangerous short-term mentality, when you have yourself convinced that you're only going to have to deal with the annoying guy once. Those people have a habit of sticking around long past their expiration dates, which is part of what makes them intolerable to begin with.

When you're trying to connect with potential clients, ask yourself this question: would I want to hang out with this person for a three-hour layover in Boise? If not, forget it. Life's too short!

A good friend of mine, a VP of a large hotel outfit in New York, told me about a recent presentation he sat through with his team. The first thing an associate asked him after the guy left was, "Would you want to have a beer with that guy?" His answer? "Hell no!"

The same theory applies when you're looking for a job! If the CEO or the person you'll be reporting to seems like a gigantic dickhead, run the other direction.

IF YOU DON'T WANT TO SPEND THREE HOURS TOGETHER IN THE MIDDLE OF NOWHERE AND HAVE A BEER WITH SOMEONE, YOU DON'T WANT TO WORK WITH HIM OR FOR HIM, EITHER.

USE CONFIDENCE, NOT INTIMIDATION

Are you cool enough, without being too cool? Confident, but not cocky? Assertive, but not aggressive? Strong, but not intimidating? If you come off as overly confident, you're instantly unapproachable, and people will assume you have too much going on to bother with them. No one wants to do business with a self-important a-hole.

CONFIDENT

Liking yourself

Willing to learn

Understanding personal shortcomings

Being humble

Being grateful

Demonstrating good character

COCKY

Thinking you are better

Being a know-it-all

Being blind to their own faults

Acting arrogant

Acting entitled

Telling you why they are so great

> BE APPROACHABLE AND
> YOU WON'T COME OFF AS A DICK.

THE NAYSAYER

When I started my professional career, I worked with a naysayer. You know the type who just disagrees with you for the sake of argument? It didn't matter what I said; she was always right. Something as immaterial as, "I can't believe this is Sandra Bullock, it doesn't even look like her" gets the response, "Oh, yes it does. That's totally Sandra Bullock." So fucking annoying. We shared an office, so naturally this got old, really fast.

It became clear after a few months that she wasn't going to change, so I talked to my reliable therapist about it. At my wits' end, I said: "It's going to have to be me or her. If we're both in this environment any longer, I might have to move my office to the custodial closet." My therapist's advice surprised me, but it was spot on. "Don't argue with this person or even try to challenge anything she says, just agree. 'Yes, you are right' to every opinion she has. These types of people like to start an argument, but when they have nowhere to go, they get burnt out." It worked! She grew flustered when I agreed with everything she said. It annoyed her that I wouldn't argue. Classic.

AGREE WITH NAYSAYERS.
THEY LOSE THEIR LEVERAGE QUICKLY.

COCKBLOCKERS

If you're too lazy to check the footnote for a full description (I get it), the Wikipedia definition of this term is:

Cockblock is a slang term for an action, intentional or not, that serves to prevent someone from having sex. Such behavior is often motivated by jealousy, or competitiveness, although it is sometimes accidental, or inadvertent. A cockblock or cockblocker is a person who engages in such obstruction or intervention.[42]

There are all kinds of cockblockers— even people who can get in the way of doing business. You simply have to get around them, or beat them at their own game. Cockblockers are a barrier to success.

A COCKBLOCKER:

- Takes credit for your deal;
- Wants all the success for him/herself;
- Excludes you from meetings;
- Doesn't give you any feedback when you're talking to them;
- Leads by negativity;
- Puts themselves up by putting others down;
- Points the finger.

Sound familiar?

STEER CLEAR OF COCKBLOCKERS, OR INTRODUCE THEM TO DOUCHEBAGS.

---

42 https://en.wikipedia.org/wiki/Cockblock

CHAPTER 14

DO it RiGHt: Hit THe C-SPot

THE BIG "O"

It is almost impossible to say no to someone who is passionate. Picture the scene in *When Harry Met Sally*, when Meg Ryan faked an orgasm in Katz's Deli and the other customer said, "I'll have what she's having!" If you are passionate enough, people want whatever it is you are offering (especially if it's a table-slapping, public orgasm).

What gives you genuine pleasure? What leaves you feeling satisfied and accomplished? If you're passionate, it's an organic conversation, not a scripted pitch. When you are genuinely excited, you give off that positive energy and leave others thirsty for the same pleasure. It's a business orgasm.

Your environment counts. Motivation is a two-way street. The people around you will either help or hinder your success. While you can't always control who you work with (unless you're the boss, and even then, not all the time), you should assess the situation and identify who is on the same page as you. Again, find the associates who get fired up about the same things you do. They're the ones who will inspire you to greatness.

PASSION + PLEASURE = GETTING OFF AND CLOSING DEALS!

FIND THE RUSH

What gives you an adrenaline high? For some people, it's crack (not okay), weed (becoming okay), or even an extreme sport (totally mainstream), but mine is making a connection with people (cooler than school). Making connections is my version of being high. I get the same adrenaline rush that people talk about getting when they skydive, or bungee jump, or summit a mountain. It's thrilling and challenging to figure out how the hell I'm going to connect with someone, sometimes in a matter of seconds. I get off on bringing people together and watching the sparks fly, knowing I am responsible. They're having a big love affair, and it's because of me.

Tapping into people's emotions and understanding what makes them tick is my gift, and being a sounding board is something that excites me. Somehow, subconsciously, I have the ability to read people. I see it all; there's nowhere to hide!

GET HIGH EVERY DAY: LOVE WHAT YOU DO.

BEING FANTAMULOUS!

"A girl should be two things: classy and fabulous."
—COCO CHANEL

We've seen this word before. I use it all the time. I can't help it! Here's how it goes: Fantastic + Tami + Fabulous = Fan-TAM-u-lous. Pick a name, add fun adjectives, combine, voila. Instant fun. Does it get any better than that? I doubt it.

I really believe in being a little fantamulous. When you put effort into what you look like, not only do you feel more confident, people notice. I might be a product of *Sex and the City*, but I honestly think I was *Sex and the City* **before** *Sex and the City*. Being fantamulous has nothing to do with your figure, age, sex, race, sexual orientation, etc.; it has to do with taking pride in how you present yourself.

Someone said to me once, "What magazine did you just step out of?" Yummy, yummy. I ate that compliment up, better than cake! Compliments work both ways; I know I can win one over, but I can be won over, too! It all starts with equal parts confidence and humility. It's about making an impression that lasts a lifetime. It's worth it; trust me. Let's all be fucking fantamulous! Now, that's a movement we should get behind.

How you present yourself directly correlates to the pride you take in your work. You don't have to follow business attire rules, but you better own what you wear! Try not being too formal. For the most part, I've stopped wearing pencil skirts and high heels — that look can be intimidating, and I want to be approachable for both men and women. I can get away with wearing jeans, my favorite tokidoki t-shirt, riding boots, and a blazer, because I wear what I feel the most confident in at that moment. And I'll admit, I can be a bombshell, or I can be a hot mess, but I try to save those looks for the weekend and keep them outside the boardroom.

A good way to start being fantamulous is to pretend you're getting ready for a first date. How much effort do you put into that? Just think about it—a business meeting could be better then the first date because, if all goes well, you'll get paid for it. (Unless you're a hooker, of course, which I don't recommend, although my favorite movie is *Dangerous Beauty*, where the courtesans are advisors to the court in the 1500s, so I can see making the rare exception.)

Being fantamulous is about more than what you wear (although, that's an important piece)! It's about your energy output. People love being around you, and you need to own it. You are the IT person. Do you know any fabulous people who don't exude confidence and positive energy? I highly doubt it.

HOW TO FAN-TAMI-FY YOUR DAY:

- ❈ Compliment others;
- ❈ Let people know when you are thinking about them;
- ◐ Smile;
- ❀ Be grateful;
- ♡ Be gracious;
- ✉ Buy gifts for no reason;
- ❊ Be a leader by taking charge;
- ✐ Include everyone. Titles are irrelevant; and
- ✉ Go to first base on every encounter.

I was with one of my most successful and best girlfriends the other day, and we passed the Drybar. She said, "You know, I am a huge customer of theirs. For $50, I can pop in there whenever I have an event or a trip. My hair looks great, I feel good, I look tailored, and I am more confident when I need to deliver. It seems worth it!" I said, "Of course. You feel fantamulous!" What an amazing concept. Not to mention, a smart woman founded Drybar. She fucking nailed it!

CREATE PERSONAL WAYS
TO MAKE THINGS FUN AND FEEL GOOD.

TOAST TO THE **FUTURE**

I'm a big believer in celebrating the small victories along the way. If you meet someone you want to work with, celebrate! Toast to your children, toast to their shoes, toast to seeing them again—just celebrate! Pre-celebrating sends the message that you're excited to see where this relationship will go. Do you need a reason to drink champagne? Celebrating yourself is reason enough.

As an angel investor and advisor, I meet a lot of young entrepreneurs. They have many hurdles and challenges, so every step closer they get to making a company successful should be celebrated. If it's with a glass of champagne or just a pat on the back, acknowledging our progress is a way to keep us motivated.

CELEBRATE THE SMALLEST OF ACHIEVEMENTS. IF COFFEE IS FOR CLOSERS, CHAMPAGNE IS FOR OPENERS!

CHAPTER 15

FAILIN' UP

THE **POWER** OF PERSUASION

Back to the C-student in me . . . the fact is, I didn't even get into San Diego State University the first time I applied. I must have been in serious denial because I thought I was, at least, smart enough to get into a top ten party school! How was this even possible? Let's see here: my GPA was a joke, I was horrible at test-taking, and the SAT scared the living shit out of me.

I had to have a course of action. I couldn't go back to high school, so my options were somewhat limited. My immediate goals were simple: I wanted to hang out with my friends at San Diego State and have the whole away-at-college experience—drink too much, gain the freshman 15+—the whole enchilada.

How could I do this as quickly as possible without taking more tests or studying? Ahhhhh, if only my grades were slightly better. What if . . . I could convince one of my high school teachers to go back and change a grade from a C to a B? Just one tiny, small tweak was all I needed to get into the prestigious, coveted, unobtainable SDSU (it's a STATE school, people!) and join my friends.

So, I did what I do best. I used my personality and charm to persuade my teacher to change my grade. Why would any reasonable teacher not want her student to go on to receive a college education? I am sure she assumed, after all of her efforts, and putting her career on the line, that I would eventually graduate with a degree! No such luck.

DON'T UNDERESTIMATE THE POWER OF PERSUASION.

MY SANDWICH BOARD

When I was a talent manager, I was working for free because my clients weren't nailing the jobs. Nonetheless, they always got access to the right meetings. When holiday season came around, they bought me Prada bags and other juicy accouterments as a thank you. Lord knows where they got the cash to pay for some of this stuff! I always pictured how funny it would be to wear a sandwich board that said, "Will work for Prada."

We all need to make money to pay the bills. Getting people access to the right meetings doesn't guarantee they will get the job, but it's still a foot in the door. When people do something nice for you, remember you're on the right track!

It's okay to work for couture instead of cash, just so long as you're moving in the right direction.

MY FIRST MILLION-DOLLAR DEAL

I had just opened the doors of my talent management company, HMG, when I met an interesting writer/actor. He had a series deal with Sony Television for a show he had created. The cheery Texan was making a decent living as a radio talk show host when he was baited like Nemo with Hollywood fame. He flipped and flopped like a fish out of water and was nearly gutted by the industry. When we sat down to discuss his desire to write, create, and star in his own series, I realized three things:

1 The producers involved were taking him to the cleaners;

2 Both he and his show had enormous potential; and

3 There was no way I could mentally fuck him up any more than he already was.

He was in a deep, dark place for no reason. He had created something amazing and was *this close* to signing his rights away, without even a glimmer of a promise that he would be a part of the project once the deal was done. It was totally unfair. And that really pissed me off.

I said, "Listen, you could take the deal and potentially lose everything, or you could take a chance with me and trust that I can find you a better deal—one that doesn't force you to sign it all away." (This is where speaking with confidence and authority is so important.)

I meant and believed everything I told him that day. Admittedly, though, I had not mapped out a strategy. I was 25 and a first-time entrepreneur. For all I knew, we would both end up eating peanut butter and jelly sandwiches for the next three years. But that day, HMG took on a client with a shitty studio deal. Fucking nailed it; I thought to myself, both impressed and elated.

Then it hit me. I realized I had never sold a TV series, never represented writers, and didn't have the vaguest idea how I would get this guy a meeting at any network. I'd just have to figure it out.

Step One: What don't I know?

Step Two: Who do I know who knows what I don't know?

Joe (not Blow), the VP of Fox television, happened to be a former actor I had represented when I was at the TPA Talent Agency. I reached out, hoping to catch up over sushi and sake, and perhaps casually pitch my show. We spent some time reminiscing, and when our bond was reaffirmed, I was comfortable enough to share the details of the project. Despite the fact that this was my one and only shot, I kicked into selling mode effortlessly.

He was intrigued. He inquired about other potential offers. I was honest. "The show is set up at Sony, but we're not happy." Simple and to the point. Read, "Whaddya got for me?"

Holy shit! The next day he called with an offer. Respectable? Yes. What we wanted? No. This was dicey. I had to decline politely without appearing ungrateful. Frankly, an extra $100K wasn't enough for my client to walk away from his Sony contract and to tarnish the relationship. Joe from Fox didn't take my response sitting down. About 15 minutes later, he scheduled a meeting with the chairman of the network. The ante was upped, and the stakes were high. This needed to be the mother of all pitches, because if we didn't land a deal, it was back to square one.

Of course, I spent some time deciding what to wear. I wanted to look professional, but hot—but not too hot—all while faking that I could afford to wear couture. My only concern was my client's delivery (and, frankly, I was worried about what he was wearing. Not many people have my sense of style.) I know I can sell, but what impression would the Texan make with the CHAIRMAN of FOX? Too late to prep him now, we'd just have to go with it. The endorphins raced through my body as I worked my magic in the room that day.

When we left, I felt like I'd put my entire life savings on black at the roulette table and walked away with the wheel still spinning. I had to wait until I got back to my office to find out where the little ball landed. Pure torture.

A million dollars later, my client was the show's creator, executive producer, and the star of the show! My Texan got the deal he deserved, and I got the validation and confidence to hit the ground running.

 USE BEGINNER'S LUCK MENTALITY.

SUPERPOWERS

Superman can fly. Flash can run so fast he breaks the sound barrier. What's your superpower? Don't worry, I'm not expecting you to shoot webs from your wrists like Spider-Man—but what do you do well? What do you do better than the next person? What differentiates you in this world? What's your unfair advantage? Your superpower can be an interest, something that comes naturally, or a skill set you've developed over time. Regardless of what "it" is, it's the thing that is at your core, your niche, and your passion. You're as protective of it as you are dedicated to strengthening it. Now, it's time to capitalize on it.

What if you don't know what your superpower is? Then, it's time for a little self-exploration.

MAKE LISTS:

★ What do you do well?
★ What do you like to do?
★ What fires you up?
★ What do you want to change about the world?
☆ What could you spend hours doing?
★ What sets you apart from your peers?
✳ What would your career be if money or qualifications were not factors?

Sometimes we overlook what comes naturally. One might incorrectly assume his or her natural traits are typical of any educated, well-adjusted individual. Guess what? They're not. For example, I thought my superpower was simply "good communication skills," which I assumed was universal. Not true. As I examined my environment, I learned that this was a valuable tool across multiple careers, and it made me unique. So I zeroed in on the superpower and perfected it until it was applicable and adaptable wherever I go.

Your superpower is your career capital; it's what makes you an asset. How does it translate to multiple fields? Communicative superpowers are extremely transferable: sales, marketing, education, writing, and politics are just a few fields where communications masters thrive. Anyone can learn job requirements; be trained to use company-specific software, or learn the curriculum they need to teach. But if you are a super-communicator, you are more than a quiz at the end of a training session. You are more than the degree you earned and the title next to your name.

People who are in tune with their superpowers are the ones that inspire others; they're the ones taking risks that lead to success. If you're in touch with your superpower, you're operating on a different level than mere mortals, and will attain your goals at lightning speed. You won't accept a position and do "just enough" to get by at work. You'll make *who you are* applicable in the workplace.

This is universal—know what you do well and incorporate it into your world every day. Don't hide it or dumb it down; instead, enhance it, nourish it, and use it to your full advantage to challenge yourself. Remember who you are, not what you were hired to do. You're not a robot nor do you want to become one.

I've been an entrepreneur for most of my career. Entrepreneurs are unique, but each has a similar blueprint of quirky characteristics that makes being their own boss more of a necessity than a choice. If you do take a job working for someone else, try to navigate like an entrepreneur in a corporate environment. If you don't, you are at risk of losing your superpower.

No one is a pro at everything, so just as important as identifying your superpower is the ability to know when and how to surround yourself with the right team. This means, asking for help and forcing your ego to take a back seat. Develop the ability to know and accept that you aren't the expert all the time. The most successful people know they don't know everything and continue to learn. The minute you stop learning, you stop growing. The moment you stop growing, you can no longer adapt to change or enhance your skill set, which is kryptonite in business.

Don't overlook what comes naturally. It's likely your calling

UNDERDOG

People like to root for the underdog so if you're smaller than your competition, use it to your advantage. Smaller is a synonym for "more agile." If you're new to an industry, being "young and hungry" is a benefit. But don't just tell them—show them!

Your youth and size allow you to give clients more attention than the bigger shops. You can put your top people on the project, and your client's complete satisfaction is your only goal. Scrappers are more creative out of necessity. Why do you think there are so many successful feel-good movies about the underdog? Because everyone likes to see them win! *Rocky*, *Jerry McGuire*, *Slumdog Millionaire*, *Rudy*, and *Seabiscuit*—you get the drift.

UNDERDOGS FIGHT HARDER
USE YOUR STATUS, NO MATTER WHAT IT IS.

THE OUTLIER

The dictionary definition of an **outlier** is something or someone that is situated away from or classed differently from a main or related body. An outlier is someone who stands apart from others of his or her group, as by behaving differently. Synonyms: nonconformist, maverick, original, eccentric.[43]

I've never approached anything I do by following the rules. As an entrepreneur, I didn't see roadblocks; I just figured out how to get the meetings I needed as I went along. My ignorance, confidence, passion, and eccentricity drove me in any and all directions until I got where I needed to be.

When I was at a new company, the term "outlier" was often applied to me. After setting up a few C-Suite meetings, the head of the division said, "I don't know how you get the meetings you do. I know it works, but I am struggling. You're an outlier, and I don't know what box to put you in."

And there it is, folks! Someone wanted to put me in a box. Shoot me in the head, please.

Why, if what someone is doing works and they are getting results, would you want to take away their superpowers? This new boss was a classic stiletto stomper. I knew she wanted to put me six feet under. The only time someone is going to put me in a box is when I die, and that box better be Gucci!

THINK DIFFERENTLY.
BE A MAVERICK—THE LARA CROFT
OF BUSINESS DEVELOPMENT.

---

43 http://www.merriam-webster.com/dictionary/outlier

FORREST GUMP

My family has called me Forrest Gump for years. They joke that I could be penniless and still have lunch with the President of the United States. Maybe it's my irrepressible optimism? I honestly don't even know how some of these crazy opportunities present themselves, but I am happy they do!

We all bitch about work but I try to avoid getting caught up in the typical woes (not enough money, underappreciated or underutilized, exhausted, and stressed out all the time). Business development can be a grind, but are you fucking kidding me? The killer expense account alone allows me to travel the world and meet the most incredible people.

Once, we had a meeting at the Olympic Headquarters in Lausanne, Switzerland. They picked us up in the official Olympic Mercedes sedan with tinted windows—the whole nine yards. The Olympic campus is beyond chic. It's on Lake Geneva (my namesake!) with the most insane public art exhibit. We ate lunch in their fabulous commissary, which served wine (all commissaries should serve wine!) at lunch. Side note: you close deals when you are drinking, business duh'velopment 101! At this point, I didn't even give a shit if we won the business on that trip; it was just so exciting to be an Olympic VIP.

When we were in the meeting, we were being total schnorrers[44] and stocking up on all of the collectible freebees around the boardroom table: official Olympic notepads, pens, and candies. It was like we needed to prove to our friends and family that we were actually there!

---

44 **Schnorrer** (שנאָרער; also spelled *shnorrer*) is a Yiddish term meaning "beggar" or "sponger".[1] (https://en.wikipedia.org/wiki/Schnorrer)

On another trip, we brought a client to the 24-hour race at Le Mans, France. Steve McQueen, baby! I thought I was the shit. Shit, I was the shit! In attendance was my favorite client, my favorite associate, and me. I arranged for VIP tickets and amazing seats in the viewing room above the track, but nothing could have prepared me for what happened next. Turns out, my client was friends with an owner of Aston Martin, pause for reaction . . . I was pinching myself! How the hell did we get so damn lucky? He gave us all-access passes to the owner's lounge where the racers ate, the official Aston Martin hospitality tent, and the racing pit. Whoa!

We rented the top floor of a house about a mile away, and the owners lived on the ground floor. They only spoke French, so we couldn't communicate with them at all. One night, we came back starving and drunk and tried to use the English/French dictionary they provided to ask them for a croissant. Yeah. *Croissant* in French is *croissant*!

For all intents and purposes, we were running around Le Mans like we were auto-racing royalty. When the race came to an end, and Aston Martin, sadly, lost, we rode off into the sunset to the after party on a golf cart with the owner and his wife.

Celebrity parties, movie premiers, yachts in Cannes, lunch with the President, tour busses with rock stars, my list goes on. Who am I? Oh yeah, Forrest Gump!

SOMETIMES THE EXPERIENCES ARE WORTH THE EVERYDAY GRIND.
KEEP IT IN PERSPECTIVE.

FAILING UP

"The one thing all famous authors, world-class athletes,
business tycoons, singers, actors, and celebrated achievers in
any field have in common is that they all began their journeys
when they were none of these things."
—MIKE DOOLEY

Rejection, failure, and disappointment—these are things that you will inevitably face throughout your career—and your life, for that matter. You must be willing to take risks, knowing you might fail. If you want to succeed, rejection is something you use to become stronger; it is not a reminder of how much you suck.

The most successful, attractive, hilarious, and amazing people I've ever met have been rejected, time and time again. When I represented actors, part of my job was to break the news when they didn't get a certain role. The first question was always "Why? What's wrong with me?" The truth is there's nothing wrong. Okay, maybe they were too blonde or had blue eyes instead of brown. The reasons were superficial and had absolutely nothing to do with their acting ability.

We have to have thick skin and accept that sometimes things don't work out or may not be the best fit, and move on. It's not a lifetime rejection from the world if someone doesn't want to work with you. Your perception of yourself is always magnified when it's a negative one. You view yourself as a failure, but that's not how others see you. Take your ego and internal voices out of the game. There are usually several reasons as to why you aren't winning the business—most of which are totally out of your control, and frankly, probably have nothing to do with you.

For example:

Loyalty: Past relationships often trump new connections. One day, someone will be loyal to you, too.

Nepotism: Maybe they have a cousin or a friend in the business? Who said life was fair?

Contractual Obligation: There could be a contract in place that the client didn't acknowledge when she approached you.

There will be times when you are lucky enough to get feedback, but when you're left hanging, let it go; you don't have a crystal ball, you're not a mind reader, and obsessing over it won't win you business. Get right back out there after you've been rejected. Don't forget that part of this is about being a player in a game. Do two things after you fail:

1 - Assess what you've learned; and

2 - Let it go.

Take risks, because in my experience, only the risk-takers win. I promise you, if you approach enough people and build enough relationships, you will get the business.

I was devastated when I had to walk away from a company I built a few years ago. It felt like I had lost my whole identity. How would I promote myself if I just failed at my own company? How would I get back on my feet? I was the CEO of nothing. I felt like a loser. I questioned if I had anything to offer the business community. What was I even worth? I was humiliated, but the outside world didn't see it the same way I did.

Hitting that low with my self-esteem and taking a deep look at myself gave me the clearest perspective I've ever had. After scraping myself off of the floor, I was forced to dig deep and find my superpower. I did a self-assessment, and the consistent theme was, "I can get to anyone." It was a reminder that no matter what I'm selling, whether it is a TV show idea, a tangible product, or a service, I know how to get in the room.

People are inspired generally by (and envious of) the risks entrepreneurs take. Being willing to put everything on the line for something you believe inspires others and earns their respect, no matter what the outcome. You're celebrated—praised, even! People do root for the underdog.

We can all fail upwards; it's just hard to see when you're failing. You can control how you are perceived. Remember, you're not alone on your journey. Go back to your mentors, friends, and family, and let them bring you back up!

—Zig Ziglar-ism[45]—

"IT'S NOT HOW HARD YOU FALL, BUT HOW HIGH YOU BOUNCE THAT COUNTS."

45 **Hilary Hinton «Zig» Ziglar** (November 6, 1926 – November 28, 2012) was an American author, salesman, and motivational speaker. (https://en.wikipedia.org/wiki/Zig_Ziglar)

TAMI-ISMS: THE CHEAT SHEET

GOOD GRADES DON'T EQUAL BUSINESS SUCCESS.

C-STUDENTS **FIGHT HARDER.**

THE **SCHOOL OF LIFE** OFFERS **THE BEST DEGREE.**

You can **blame the men** for coming up with a universal scoring system **to rate people's beauty.**

FINISH SCHOOL. ☺

STATISTICALLY SPEAKING, WOMEN TEND TO HAVE HIGHER EQ THAN MEN. **HA!**

Practice self-awareness. The ability to stand outside yourself and look in is invaluable for personal growth and relationship-building.

ALWAYS CARRY **DOUBLE-SIDED TAPE** IN YOUR PURSE.

BE POPULAR FOR THE RIGHT REASONS.

Be nice to everyone. You never know who the gatekeeper is.

BE A CARETAKER AND SMOTHER THOSE AROUND YOU WITH **L♥VE.**

LET OTHERS INVEST IN YOUR SUCCESS. **YOUR MENTORS ARE FOR LIFE.**

Laughing is productive.

➡ BE ACCESSIBLE. KEEP IT SIMPLE. ⬅

PREPARATION IS ESSENTIAL. DON'T WALK INTO THE ROOM LOOKING LIKE A NINCOMPOOP.

SHUT UP AND LISTEN TO THE CLIENTS' NEEDS. PUT ELECTRICAL TAPE ON YOUR MOUTH, IF YOU MUST.

Get involved in something bigger than yourself. The rewards are bigger than your paycheck, and you never know what muckety-muck might be involved, too.

CLOSING THE DEAL IS THE SAME PROCESS AT WORK AS IT IS AT HOME. BUT WHEN YOU'RE AT WORK, **KEEP IT CLEAN!**

YOUR PARTIES ARE A DIRECT REFLECTION OF WHO YOU ARE AND HOW YOU DO BUSINESS. TAKE IT UP A NOTCH.

Every encounter is an opportunity. Reframe a "no" into a "hello"!

YOU'RE ONLY AS STRONG AS THE PEOPLE AROUND YOU.

IF YOU WANT TO KEEP YOUR AUDIENCE ENGAGED, **BE ENTHUSIASTIC WHEN SPEAKING!**

Take some initiative and **line up a meeting already!**

INCLUDE THE BUYER IN THE PROCESS.

Be creative in how you present yourself to potential employers to **stand out from the pack.**

NEVER leave a meeting ~without~ **making your ask.**

BE PRESENT WHEN YOU ARE PHYSICALLY PRESENT —AS IN YOU CAN PINCH ME.

BE AWARE OF THE NONVERBAL SIGNALS YOU ARE SENDING.

NEVER PROMISE PERFECTION.

AFFECTION BREAKS THE ICE.

Good business development executives are rare.

USE WHATEVER IT TAKES TO GET IN THE ROOM.

"**Yes**" opens doors.

Seize the moment to connect with people **before the moment's gone.**

SHOW 'EM YOU AREN'T AFRAID OF A CHALLENGE.

Make your product attractive with creative positioning.

DITCH THE PITCH.

Everyone loves a winner.

BE FLEXIBLE TO BE SURE YOU ARE MEETING **THE CLIENT'S NEEDS** AND NOT YOUR OWN

If you want a seat at the table, take it.

DON'T SQUANDER EXPENSIVE OPPORTUNITIES TO CONNECT. GET OUT THERE AND MINGLE.

Let your clients boost your sales acumen by donating to your future success.

IT'S ALWAYS GOOD TO HAVE AN **ICEBREAKER** –PLANNED OR UNPLANNED. **TURN** AN **EMBARRASSING MOMENT** INTO AN **OPPORTUNITY** TO PUT **EVERYONE AT EASE.**

WE ARE ALL CREATED EQUAL.

Sometimes the joke is on you.
You have to be able to laugh at your own expense.

BE THE FIRST TO LET GO AND HELP OTHERS FEEL SAFE. BE SILLY, HAVE FUN, BUST A MOVE.

DON'T TAKE YOURSELF TOO SERIOUSLY.

OWN YOUR MISTVKES.

BE THE BIGGER PERSON AND TAKE CHARGE OF AWKWARD ENCOUNTERS.

Avoidance does not make an issue disappear; it only drives others to *make assumptions* based on incomplete information.

WRITE YOUR DREAM OBITUARY, AND THEN LIVE IT!

♥ The importance of foreplay cannot be overstated. ♥

Attract positive attention by rooting for others' success.

ALL IT TAKES IS JUST ONE SMILE TO CHANGE THE ENERGY IN A ROOM.

EMOTIONAL ECSTASY

is totally legal in all 50 states.

Free publicity. Priceless.

A little flattery **will get you everywhere.**

MAKE EVERYONE FEEL LIKE A BILLION BUCKS AND SHOW THEM YOUR APPRECIATION FOR HOW THEY MAKE YOU FEEL.

PUT ON YOUR BIG GIRL PANTIES AND **SUCK IT UP.**

Learn something personal about everyone you meet. Your acquaintance-to-relationship conversion rate will skyrocket.

Approach each client as if you're the only game in town. If you've made the clients' needs your top priority, the competition doesn't stand a chance anyway.

A positive pipeline is a business development executive's best friend.

SOMETIMES JUST BEING A GIRL LENDS ITSELF TO TAKING ONE FOR THE TEAM.

ALWAYS ACCEPT OFFERS OF HELP, EVEN IF YOU DON'T NEED IT YET.

HAVE AN UNLIMITED SPENDING ACCOUNT BY MAKING PEOPLE FEEL GOOD.

FOCUS ON THE RESULTS, NOT THE PROCESS *(but don't tell your boss I said so)*.

YOU CAN BE A NEGATIVE ASSHOLE, BUT THEN YOU HAVE TO LIVE WITH YOURSELF, AND YOU'LL HAVE NO FRIENDS.

Create a circle of trust.

Connect people with the right contacts, so they can succeed too.

Show people how much you appreciate them by going the extra mile.

WHEN APPROACHING A NEGATIVE SITUATION, **ALWAYS BEGIN WITH REASSURANCE.**

It is possible to be sweet with an edge, like Sour Patch Kids.

OWN WHO YOU ARE, WHICH IS FANTAMULOUS. LET'S RUN THIS MOTHA!

NO RISK, NO REWARD.

MEN NEED SHOULDERS TO CRY ON TOO, YOU KNOW. BE THERE WITH BEER.

Ladies, use your inherent superior emotional intelligence to demand equal pay.

YOU'RE ONLY BEING USED IF YOU DON'T GET ANYTHING IN RETURN.

WHEN you get hit on at work, nip it in the bud swiftly and gracefully!

All is fair in love and war —and busine$$.

Be cool, *even when your favorite outfit gets destroyed.*

FACE YOUR FEARS, NO MATTER HOW TERRIFYING THEY MAY BE.

You're never too old to work it.

DON'T SECOND-GUESS YOUR STRENGTHS.

Feeling vulnerable is inherently **human.**

★ HIGH—LEVEL POSITIONS CAN BE ISOLATING. NO ONE WANTS TO FEEL ALONE. ★
MAKE IT YOUR DUTY TO KEEP THE TOP DOGS COMPANY.

*Let others know that **you hear them**
and that their **feelings are valid.***

BE REALISTIC ABOUT WHO YOU ARE,
AND, REMEMBER, WE'RE ALL A LITTLE
FUCKED UP, FABULOUS, AND FLAWED.

"STAY TRUE TO YOURSELF,
EVEN IF YOU'RE AN ODDBALL."
(We love Diane Keaton★)

**YOUR ALTER EGO
IS GIVING YOU SOME
IMPORTANT MESSAGES**
(OR CONFUSING THE HELL OUT OF YOU).
**LISTEN TO YOUR
DUELING THOUGHTS,
BUT TRUST YOUR GUT.**

Don't torture yourself by
playing the guessing game.
Move toward the future.

SEE ALL SIDES BEFORE WEIGHTING IN
ON BUSINESS OR PERSONAL CONFLICTS
(EVEN IF IT MEANS LOSING SLEEP OVER IT).

Don't show up exhausted.
If it's the last day of an event, skip it and go straight to the airport!!!

FOCUS YOUR ENERGY ON LAYING THE GROUNDWORK.
BY THE TIME YOU'RE **IN THE ROOM, YOUR WORK SHOULD BE DONE.**

Your **behavior and etiquette
dictates the future** of the relationship.
Be a girl who knows better
and **own the room.**

**Be a person
others can rely on.**

**INSPIRE OTHERS TO SUCCEED;
IT WILL SHINE BACK ON YOU.**

In the immortal words of advertising giant Ogilvy & Mather,
"You cannot bore people into buying your product;
— you can only interest them in buying it." —

BE CLEVER, KEEP IT SHORT, AND HAVE FUN
WHEN FOLLOWING UP WITH CLIENTS.

SHOW YOU ARE HEALTHY, ENTHUSIASTIC, AND APPROACHABLE BY CUSSING WITH CLASS!

TAKE CHANCES!
IF IT DOESN'T WORK OUT, WHO GIVES A FUCK?

There is enough work for everyone. Make friends with your competitors. *They are your allies, not your enemies.*

DEVELOP PACKING RITUALS. YOUR CHOICE OF CLOTHING MATTERS; IT GIVES CLUES TO OTHERS ABOUT YOUR PERSONALITY.

Don't forget to **inspire** and remind your internal team **why they hired you.**

Above all else, **be confident and comfortable in your own skin,** *no matter where you are or who you are talking to.*

DRINKING AND POSTING CAN BE HAZARDOUS. THINK BEFORE YOU POST.

BEAUTY SLEEP IS NOT A MYTH, AND THAT GOES FOR MEN TOO!

*Politicians and CEOs know—**appearances do matter.***

WEAR SOMETHING THAT MAKES YOU FEEL BRILLIANT AND POWERFUL, *i.e.: designer glasses, Italian power suit, Yves Saint Laurent briefcase.*

IF YOU CAN HAVE LUNCH WITH A TOP EXECUTIVE, THEN YOU CAN HAVE LUNCH WITH ANYONE.

AN INFLUENCER IS ONLY AS STRONG AS HIS OR HER CONNECTIONS.

Perception is reality.

PEOPLE CAN SMELL BULLSHIT—BE AUTHENTIC.

Don't play into victims. *You're not doing them any favors.*

DON'T BE A DOUCHEBAG
THE COOLER THE PERSON, THE MORE ATTRACTIVE THEY BECOME. OR IF THEY'RE A TOOL, THE LESS ATTRACTIVE THEY BECOME.

Meet as many people as possible, whichever side of the table you are on.

If you don't want to spend three hours together in the middle of nowhere and have a beer with someone, you don't want to work with him or for him, either.

BE APPROACHABLE AND YOU WON'T COME OFF AS A DICK.

Agree with naysayers. *They lose their leverage quickly.*

Steer clear of cockblockers, OR INTRODUCE THEM TO THE DOUCHEBAGS.

PASSION + PLEASURE = GETTING OFF AND CLOSING DEALS!

Get high every day: **LOVE WHAT YOU DO**

CREATE PERSONAL WAYS TO MAKE THINGS FUN AND FEEL GOOD.

Celebrate the smallest of achievements. *If coffee is for closers, champagne is for openers!*

DON'T UNDERESTIMATE THE POWER OF PERSUASION.

It's okay to work for couture instead of cash, just so long as you're moving in the right direction.

Don't overlook **what comes naturally;** *it's likely* **your calling.**

USE BEGINNER'S LUCK MENTALITY.

UNDERDOGS FIGHT HARDER USE YOUR STATUS, NO MATTER WHAT IT IS.

Think differently. Be a maverick—the Lara Croft of business development.

Sometimes the experiences are worth the everyday grind. Keep it in perspective.

IT'S NOT HOW HARD YOU FALL,
BUT HOW HIGH YOU BOUNCE
THAT COUNTS.

— *Zig-Ziglarism* —

MY FELLOW PRINCESS GODDESS WARRIORS, I wish you an abundance of belly laughs and success! I already want to go to first base with all of you. I am so proud to be among such powerful girls. If a C-student can become POTUS and I can write a book, then I am certain EVERYONE reading this is capable of accomplishing ANYTHING they set their pretty little minds to. Go forth and kick ass!

XOXO,

-TAMI

P.S.
If you find any mistakes in the book, remember I'm a C-Student!!

ACKNOWLEDGEMENTS

✳ Jamie Posnanski, for encouraging me to share what he calls "My Magic" relationship building skills;

★ Caroline Alabi, incredibly funny and off the charts talented, who helped me early on;

✶ My amazingly brilliant editor, Brooke "Broxy" White, who fucking gets it and might be more irreverent than I am;

♡ My Mom, Phyllis Caskey, who has read the book 400,000 times and never withheld her feedback and praise;

♡ My Stepfather, Marshall "DH" Caskey, who painstakingly copy edited the book and didn't mess with my voice;

❋ My Sister-in-law, Ligia Holzman, who graciously provided her creative inspiration and a bottemless martini;

❀ Ivette Rodriguez, my rock star Puerto Rican Sister, for handling my PR;

❀ My illustrator, Rocío "To the Rescue" Hedman, for capturing my voice and bringing us a hysterical and stunning visual experience;

❋ Jennifer DAME Reitman, for her mad skills in content and digital marketing;

❀ Reeva Hunter Mandelbaum for her push, advice, confidence and a dose of reality! ;

❀ Princess Pooneh Mohajer for putting her law school degree to work again and saving my ass;

✳ Dr. Idell Natterson, my super therapist, who has been by my side for the last seven years and doesn't think I am nuts, even when she is scraping me off the floor;

★ Dr. Steve Parker, who has gotten me over many humps;

- My Womb-Mate Sean Holzman, life would be "VVVVVVery Narrow" without you;
- My OLDER Brother Danny Holzman who showed us all that we can never go too far with humor!;
- My Stepmother Corinne "Fashionista" Holzman who put the term Stepmonster out to pasture;
- My Father Bob "The Schmoozer" Holzman for my humor and salesmanship skills;
- My Sister-in-law Bettina "Everything is Better with Bacon" Holzman—the family's Celebrity!;
- My scrumptious nieces and nephew Olivia, Cassie and Jesse Holzman for making me feel loved;
- My adorable adopted sponsored Daughter Srey M., for my daily perspective;
- My gorgeous Wackpack (where to begin?) and even the occasional douchebag.

ABOUt **the author**

Tami Holzman loves to make people happy—whether that means giving a confidence boost, an introduction to that person they just can't seem to get to, or strategic counseling on a not yet fully baked idea. She is passionate about helping people succeed.

Tami was born and raised in Chatsworth, California and was always a "C" student, which really bothered her, but not enough to actually study—she was busy honing her social skills at the mall. Tami found humor was the way to compensate for her insecurities and, years later, it was her humor and self-reliance that helped her achieve professional success.

From C-Student to the C-Suite is a modern-day guide to business and relationships—showing how a girl with straight C's in school but straight A's in Emotional Intelligence became savvy in the cutthroat business world.

Tami began her career in the entertainment industry as a talent agent, show creator and executive producer, with development deals at NBC, HBO and the Fox Network. She segued into a successful career in marketing services for Fortune 500 companies.

Today, she is an angel investor, advisor, entrepreneur and brand ambassador. Tami loves to mentor and promote opportunities for women.

Tami lives in Pacific Palisades, overlooking the Pacific Ocean where you can find her hosting friends while saluting the sun with a cocktail in hand and an ever-present smile on her face.

LADiES & Gentlemen:

-TAMi HOLZMAN-

fromcstudenttothecsuite.com